HOTELS, RESORTS AND RESTAURANTS
Planning, Designing and Construction

A Facility Planning

About the Author

Prof. (Dr.) Jagmohan Negi, more than 40 years experience in academic, educational, administrative, and financial areas of Tourism & Hospitality. He started his career as Lecturer, Professor, Director, Executive Director, Consultant and Expert, Adviser. Accredited for academic planning designing management and operation of number of Institute, colleges and departments of Hospitality Management Institutes.

First academician who conducted research (PhD.) on Hospitality Management in 1972-74. First Indian author who wrote books on various subjects of Hotel Management. Authored more than 35 books and research work on tourism and hospitality, many of which are being used as text books in schools and Universities in India and Abroad.

He worked under the advice of renowned International Experts, invited by the Government of India for development and promotion of Hotel and Catering Education in India in 1960s. Widely traveled India and Abroad. Acquired national and international reputation and fame in the field of Tourism & Hospitality. Guest Professor and Speaker in more than 15 Universities in India and abroad.

Three times Award winner and Honored by the Ministry of Tourism, Government of India for his outstanding work of writing books on Tourism & Hospitality. Very acceptable and familiar person among research scholars and students.

First Director of NCHM&CT, Ministry of Tourism, Government of India. Presented and delivered number of papers as an expert in many national and international seminars and conferences. Expert, Adviser and consultant for Tourism & Hospitality Projects. Expert Member of High powered delegation to Switzerland on Hospitality Education & Research Programs on behalf of Federation of Hotel & Restaurant Associations of India (FHRAI), an apex body of 3,500 leading hoteliers of India. Founder Chairman, Himalayan Tourism and Recreation in Mountains and International Culinary Foundation, New Delhi. Fellow of Hotel Catering Institutional Management Association, London. Presently National Level Adviser: Tourism & Hospitality Education & Research.

HOTELS, RESORTS AND RESTAURANTS

Planning, Designing and Construction

A Facility Planning

Jagmohan Negi
and
Gaurav Manoher

KANISHKA PUBLISHERS, DISTRIBUTORS
NEW DELHI-110 002

KANISHKA PUBLISHERS, DISTRIBUTORS
4697/5-21A, Ansari Road, Daryaganj
New Delhi -110 002
Phones : 2327 0497, 2328 8285
Fax : 011-2328 8285
E-mail : kanishka_publishing@yahoo.co.in

First Published-2008
Edition-2013

ISBN: 978-81-8457-066-3

PRINTED IN INDIA

Published by Madan Sachdeva for Kanishka Publishers, Distributors, 4697/5-21A, Ansari Road, Daryaganj, New Delhi-110 002, Typeset by Sunshine Graphics, Delhi, and Printed at Rajdhani Printers, Delhi.

Preface

Travel and leisure is the world's largest and fastest growing industry. We anticipate the increasing demand for diverse hotels, resorts, and leisure-time amenities now appearing worldwide.

"Hotels, Resorts and Restaurants: Planning, Designing and Construction: A Facility Planning" presents the range of significant hotel types being developed today and illustrates them in their full global array of settings.

If one is to write a business plan for a venture of hotels, resorts and restaurant, one will have you to do a Feasibility Analysis before one does a business plan. Because one need to verify whether the enterprise is vialable before one spends the time and money into doing a full-blown business plan. Any information one gathers and the time one spends on the Feasibility Analysis will be directly useful in developing the business plan.

The purpose of the Feasibility Analysis is to make sure that one is on the right track. Two basic questions needs to be answered with the analysis:

1) Is there sufficient demand for the product or service?
2) Can the product or service be provided on a profitable basis?

Feasibility of hotels, restaurants and resorts for planning, designing focuses on creating, accelerating, and enhancing value for clients. Experience allows us to recommend the combination of programmes, land uses, and events that optimize resort performance.

One has to understand consumer trends, the future direction of the leisure market, and competitive resort products. This allows one to identify products, environments, and experiences to enhance clients' projects. The book provides strategic advice to maximize the economic returns of hospitality-development programmes. The projects have often focused on the programming and feasibility of hotel developments and fractional ownership.

Design, planning and construction discusses the latest trends from guestrooms perched atop ultra-tall mixed-use towers to lavish desert villas shaded by high-rise structures to exotically themed resorts rising out of pristine tropical island waters.

The book outlines essential planning and design considerations based on the latest data, supported by technical information and illustrations, including original plans. Analysis and theory supports each of the major trends that is presented, highlighting how the designer's work fits into the development of the industry as a whole, and giving a clear understanding of how successful new concepts develop.

The experienced author team and their contributors represent both the professional and academic sides of the subject. The major sections covering hotel types, design, and construction, provide information on the development, architecture, designing, and construction with a comprehensive and practical international overview of hotel design.

It includes vital technical information and covers a wide range of hotel types for comparison. Well-known author team represents both professional and academic sides of hotel design, planning and construction.

The book recognizes the standard of information. It provides and regards it as a critical role in making life easier for contractors and specialist suppliers. The ability to accept and assimilate other consultants work into a coherent, centralized package is a valuable tool to any contractor who is driven by the need for cost and quality control.

This book offers the full range of services required, from building design, internal planning including coordination of kitchen planning, furniture selection and layout, fabric, colour and bric-a-brac selection, restaurant designing, bars fitting design and product display through to external drinking areas and signage opportunities. In short, it delivers the complete package.

When a contractor leads a building team, reputations are exposed to the care and attention of others. In such situations, consultants carry a responsibility for their own practice, plus that of the lead contractor.

Hospitality facilities such as restaurants and bars/pubs hold a special place in modern day society. The modern bar/pub, a drinking house, is often more eye-catching and minimalist than the traditional pub. These establishments tend towards a cleaner, brighter atmosphere in which to eat and drink. All have their own specific requirements, some individual and some to a corporate theme. The comprehensive understanding of the functional aspects of running a bar and a pub, together with a design sensitivity that guarantees atmosphere and operational efficiency.

The main features of the book are:

- Contains an excellent overview of the hotel industry and resort properties.
- Presents line drawings and design for each and every division and section of the hotel building, guest room, restaurant, bar etc.
- Includes vital technical information on functional relationship, kitchen layout and design and facility analysis.
- Covers a wide range of hotel types for comparison.
- Explain the methods for determination of room rates with special reference to Hubbart Formula.
- The subject matter is supported by tables, figures, diagrams, line drawings, designs photographs, references, comprehensive bibliography and index.

We acknowledge our gratitude to all hotels, restaurants, bars and pubs who immensely contributed in the preparation of this book. Our heartiest thanks for the guidance and assistance received from the various architects and consulting teams who have been a constant source of inspiration for the preparation of this publication. In the end, we thank our publisher Mr. Madan Sachdeva, and his dedicated team who untiringly put their best efforts in bringing out this book in the present form.

Authors

Contents

List of Figures

List of Tables

Chapter 1

Hotels, Resorts and Restaurants: An Introduction

Profitability is the main objectives of any project investment analysis. Since the last few years many investors have started their entry into the hospitality business. Most of these investors belong to the following categories:

1) Those buying an existing hotel property.
2) Those converting private house into a full-fledged hotel.
3) Those venturing a new hotel project.

All prospective hoteliers are confronted with many problems in the initial stages of hotel operation. There are certain basic rules, which if properly followed will definitely bring profitability and a good returns on the capital invested. It would be useful to understand basic rules some of which are given below:

1) The main objective of the hotel business is that the rate of return on capital should be comparable to any other comparable investment.
2) A hotel project is built to produce the expected returns on investment.
3) The amount of investment should stay within development forecasts.
4) The market is to be dictated by the capital invested.
5) Scope for future expansion and extension should be taken into account while building the hotel. It is an

accepted fact that extension usually gives a better pro-rata return than constructing a new hotel building.

6) Efforts be made for installing labour saving devices, equipment and machinery at the start of the business.
7) The pricing policy must be economical for better return based on capital costs.

The visitors from abroad are the primary sources of business for hotels. International tourism is developing more rapidly and both government and the private sector are making substantial efforts to attract visitors from abroad. There are many ways through which hotels at little cost can cash on opportunities being offered by international tourism. Some of these methods are:

1) Contact the wholesalers to include your hotel in their package tours.
2) Cooperate with airlines and other organisations bringing foreign tourists and travel writers on familiarisation tours.
3) Make promotional material available for distribution overseas in the language the country where it is to be disseminated.
4) Special interest groups are an important source of business. Wildlife tours, adventure tours, historical sites tours, have bright possibilities.
5) Provide special promotional rates for international visitors specially encouraging them during slack periods.
6) 'Extend the invitation' by advertising in directories which are used by travel agents to increase markets in planning hotel accommodation for their clients.
7) Write directly to those overseas travel agents sending significant number of their clients.
8) Utilise the services of hotel representatives operating abroad.
9) Ask business clients to urge international groups to hold their conventions. Make a direct approach to the head of foreign associations and their convention holders.

The American Hotel and Motel Association has offered the following suggestions which are practicable while servicing international visitors:

1) Correspondence from abroad should be answered promptly and in the language of the person who has written.
2) Do something about the language problem, such as:

   (*i*) Utilise the language skill of your employees as interpreters.
   (*ii*) Provide employees and foreign guests with phrase books which have English translations for travellers, of words commonly used.
   (*iii*) Have menus available at least in French, German, English, Spanish and Hindi version.
   (*iv*) Provide for easy and fair currency exchange.
   (*v*) Make available tape recorders with foreign language tapes to be used on local tours.
   (*vi*) In handling group tours, pre-register members of the party, be sure all members of the group understand meal and tipping arrangements and that all accounts are settled before departure.

The hotel business is capital intensive in nature. The major part of the cost of building is involved in providing the bedrooms. This results in high building costs. The greater the building costs, the greater the overhead costs. Increasing costs of overhead forces a hotel to earn a large profit, as the same is required to meet overhead costs and show an acceptable return on borrowed money and equity of the owners/shareholders.

Many hotel buildings with high costs have provision for large public areas, big bedrooms, wide corridors and provision for heating and lighting. These factors will lead to higher maintenance costs, with the result the cost of building dictates to a large degree the room rates of the hotel.

Chapter 2

Hotel Building Designs

In a hotel project there are a series of design decisions which affect both the capital and operating costs. The architectural decisions affect the energy use, heat gain, heat loss and infiltration, and are little different from those for other building types, excepting that the hotel guest room tower has some unusual characteristics which help channel the alternatives in certain directions. The engineering decisions include many mechanical and electric systems, along with their flexibility and control.

The hotel architectural decisions are basically concerned with:

1) Building shape
2) Building site
3) View
4) Orientation, setting and balconies
5) Building construction and operational costs.

Building Shape

The circular form is the most efficient in terms of surface-to-volume ratio. The long rectangular slab is more efficient than the more compact, nearly square tower. Because the highly cellular nature of the guest room portion of the hotel, often comprising 65 per cent to 75 per cent of the building gross floor area, it is necessary to transform the square shape to some types of 'pinwheel', 'cruci-form', or similar cross-section to allow easy access to the individual guest rooms. Actually the corners of a pure square shape are often left void, because of the difficulty in direct corridor access. This configuration greatly reduces the relative efficiency of the vertical guest room tower and make it the least efficient.

The circular towers require the least building perimeter/room, and the ratio falls within a fairly narrow range. The horizontal slab is reasonably efficient, and the number of guest rooms per floor has little influence on the ratio of perimeter/room. On the other hand, the vertical tower shows the broadest range. The perfect square is highly efficient, however, the efficiency in terms of perimeter room, is drastically reduced the fewer. The rooms/floor (Ref. Fig. 2.17) identifies some typical design solution.

Building Site

The major architectural decision is the sitting of the structure. Actually, the shape of the building and the setting of the structure are closely related, for one building form is best sited at one orientation, and another form at the different angle. The location, view, and the orientation of the hotel affect the setting possibilities which are quite different from other commercial or residential buildings.

Location

The hotel structure will vary greatly depending on its locations. One form is appropriate in urban locations, where land costs are high and where the site shape and city grid may limit the choice of building form and orientation.

The growth in the hotel industry at airport and suburban locations, where less expensive land, height restriction and the presence of few adjacent buildings all serve to greatly, modify the hotel structure. The choice of hotel for these locations is much broader.

View

The designer will shape the building to get the maximum number of rooms oriented to take advantage of an attractive view, operators generally can and do charge a slightly higher rate for rooms with a special view.

Orientation, Setting and Balconies

The orientation of the circular tower is, of course, immaterial, however, the mechanical system may have to be more sophisticated, more expensive, because of the continually changing solar conditions as the sun moves around the building. The square shape can be turned to balance best the advantages of the South exposure with the disadvantages of the West.

The horizontal slab has definite energy saving advantages. It is bilateral plan, with only two orientations, and the end walls generally are designed without glazing, which allows the careful orientation along an East-West axis so that the rooms face South and North. The deformed square generally has rooms facing four directions and may have as such as 50 per cent more perimeter than the pure square tower, however, the shape may also provide additional shading of certain glass areas.

Commercial developers consider the construction costs on a square foot basis, while hotel developers place emphasis on knowing and comparing the gross cost per guest room, which includes a pro-rated share of all public space. The higher the cost per room, the more public facilities the hotel is likely to have, or the grandeur, the public space, or the larger and more luxurious the guest rooms.

Building Construction and Operational Costs

There are no set rules for determining the area of the land required for a hotel. The site of the hotel will depend upon the accommodation capacity required—guest rooms and restaurants, convention room and other facilities. Maximum site utilisation will involve basement and possible sub-basement construction with a high rise building occupying the maximum area of the site to the limit of density allowed. Height limitations apply to most cities as well as rural areas. In considering the most economical number of guest room per floor which affects the optimum size/height relationship of building—account must be taken of both regulatory standards and operational needs. Fire regulations and safety code standard limit the travel distances to exist staircases. A minimum of two staircase is necessary allowing

20-35 rooms on a double loaded corridor upto 50, if an automatic sprinkler system is installed. The exact number will depend on room sizes, building construction and layout, staircase positions, height, fire prevention system and on local standards. For housekeeping organisation, the number of rooms of average standard per floor, should be multiple of 14 to 16: the number which can be efficiently cleaned and serviced by room attendant. Standards governing building safety and protecting both the occupant and public are governed by legislation.

The premises must satisfy the requirements stipulated by the hotel operating company. This will include standard of size and service for guest rooms and public areas and their associated operational facilities.

The current emphasis of convention business is tending to result in the development of larger, taller and more complex hotel sites. The opposite trend is seen in many of the developing resort areas in mountain and coastal settings.

Aware of the importance of environmental conservation, new hotels are in fact clusters of low rise units arranged around central facilities. The building groups may be separated stimulating village layouts or concentrated into one part of the site to reduce the encroachment on the surrounding environment. Individual units may be stepped down or staggered, taking advantage of ground slopes, in order to provide horizontal separation and individual outlook. The pyramidal groupings may also be used to give a low profile silhouette and minimise the intrusion of the landscape. In case of resort developments, the main buildings may be of prominent, multi-storeyed designs, forming a focal point of interest and activity, whilst the individual apartmental buildings, villas, and other holidays units for family or groups use and may be individually separated or joined by terracing or linking together. Such layouts are generally set in landscaped grounds including amenity areas and recreational facilities.

The most economical layout for multi-storeyed construction is generally a linear plan with guest rooms or both sides of central corridor. Depending on the area and shape of the site the basic corridor layout may be extended and linked to form floor plans of the forms.

The last two arrangements provide scope for the use of central area as an atrium or lobby. Garden, swimming pools and other features may be constructed within the protection of the area either at the ground level or above the roof of public rooms occupying into the lower floors. Such landscaping creates an attractive aspect to the rooms facing inwards and counters the loss of external view. Thus, the hotel provides its own environment and becomes independent of surroundings. Hotel buildings can also be designed to a curred or circular plan, although these are expensive in framework construction and fillings.

The hotel business makes its money from the building. It operates on a profit margin on the products sold daily. On an average the ratio of profit on individual sales are, rooms 70 per cent, beverages 50 per cent, commercial rental 15 per cent and on food a very little percentage.

Out of the total cost, 65 per cent goes into the public and service areas, and 35 per cent into rooms. The non-profit areas must be there to rent the room, rooms alone fail to meet the main demand of customers' food, lodging and entertainment.

The following are some rules from extensive hotel research and study based on 65 per cent occupancy break-even point:

1) Room construction cost should not exceed Rs.1,00,000 per Rs.100 average room rate.
2) The cost of land should not exceed 10 per cent of the cost of the building.
3) The number of necessary employees should not exceed the number of rentable rooms.
4) Bedrooms (total floor area) should be at least slightly larger than public and service areas; and the more the better conditioned by those three basic demands again.

The planning, designing and construction of hotel is known as 'integration'. The design creates a lively atmosphere which sets the scene for hotel facilities and services. The modern day travellers seek 'experience' and more conveniences. The architects and designers create an ambience throughout the hotel premises. It begins with the exterior, is carried to the lobby and public areas, and continues to the guest rooms and usually reaches its peak in the speciality restaurant and night clubs.

Designer Henry End of the USA says that two-thirds of the hotel rooms in service today is dull and drab without charm. Architect E. Hennessy points out that changes in the means of transportation, vocation, and methods of conducting business, are creating new needs in hotel facilities.

The hotel history is full of examples of pool planning and construction. For example, in the Caribbean area, one large hotel built a second pool when it found that the original one was shaded all the time by the hotel itself.

There has been cases where hotels have been built with only a few hundred guest rooms to occupy conventional facilities for more than a thousand, and without the ability to expand.

In a large hotel in Pennsylvania with function space for several thousand, on a single floor, no good toilet facilities are available on that floor !

The worst blunder occurred many years ago, when it was discovered, only a few days before a new hotel was opened, that the architect had failed to provide for a kitchen !

The important question is, what does the public want or need? Ignoring what the public wants or needs can be very costly.

A major hotel in the USA had to spend nearly $ 300,000 a few years after it was built to add a swimming pool not originally planned.

According to Morris Lapidus, noted hotel architect, responsible for some of Miamis most glamorous edifies, hotel guests fall into two categories:

1) Business travellers
2) Pleasure travellers.

The business travellers want a comfortable bed, easy accessible closet and drawers, space, good lighting for reading, excellent lighting for make-up or sharing and fast service.

The leisure travellers appreciate all these necessities, but above all, they want the atmosphere of their hotel and room, to reflect the ambience of the city or country in which they are visiting without detracting from the quality of the service. They want to feel as though they really are away from home.

Thus both groups of travellers expect something different in the hotel than they all find at home.

Now-a-days there is little demand from travellers for the 'home away from home' type of accommodation. Lapidus further states, "the effort to capture the feeling of home in a hotel room is futile and expensive." Today, the hotelier should be guided by what will give him maximum occupancy with minimum maintenance cost.

Figures 2.2, 2.3, 2.4 and 2.5 show the various types of hotel plan.

Multi-Storeyed High Rise Buildings

High rise buildings are suitable for city centres or resort developments were site costs or area restrictions necessitate the concentration of the building to obtain the maximum site density. The plan area of public and service levels is usually greater than that covered by the multi-storeyed guest room slab and may extend out to form a broad base or podium or to be bounded on two or more sides, such as within an atrium.

Layout planning in both public and service areas is affected by the methods by which drainage and support are given to the guest rooms floors above. The obstructive effect of large numbers of columns, penetrating these areas may be solved in several ways; for example, number of columns in the guest room structure can be greatly reduced by central positioning or by using structural cross walls and/or spine walls (e.g. between bathroom and bedroom areas), the supporting structure under the multi-storeyed slab may form a shadow pad and extend up into the structural cross walls above, the multiple loads from above can be redistributed by longitudinal beams, extending the full depth of intermediary service floor, the guest room, tower may be supported mainly from a central core structure which also provides an enclosure for vertical services and circulation.

The various forms of high rise building are given in Figures 2.5 to 2.17.

Circulation Pattern

In considering the flow patterns of guest arrivals, departure and usage of hotel facilities, it is necessary to take into account the location of the hotel, the nature of the business, the main modes of transport for guest arrivals and departures and the internal circulations of guests and staff. The routes taken by guests, non-resident customers and staff tend to follow distinct patterns and these establish clear relationship between the various areas of the hotel. The layout must facilitate convenient and efficient circulation, and provide separate toilets for guests, staff and service personnel. Circulation planning in multi-building projects is an essential step in determining the layout of the development, the phases for extension and economic feasibility.

As an important aspect of inter-relationship planning, areas which are associated in use or function must be identified and linked or grouped together. The facilities and services required in each of the areas must also be indicated. The more numerous the movements, the closer the areas should be located together. The circulation pattern and the relationships could be shown by use of flowchart or diagrams as given in Figure 2.1. These diagram/charts establishes the route of circulation. It does not show the relative importance of each link. Areas which could be grouped together to facilitate frequent inter-movement of large numbers of people is the area between reception foyer and banquet or convention hall; and areas for rapid service or efficient working as in the kitchen layout. There are other distances which are less significant, provided this is not monotonously prolonged but the cost and space utilisation may be predominant.

The answer to how to build today for tomorrow is to build structures that are adaptable to what our guest would like to have. Not what we would like to see, not what are architects feel is necessary, but what are public's wants. (Ref. Wayne B. Duddle stin, President Text-Craft Builders, Inc., AH & MA convention, Maimi Beach, Florida, December 10, 1965.)

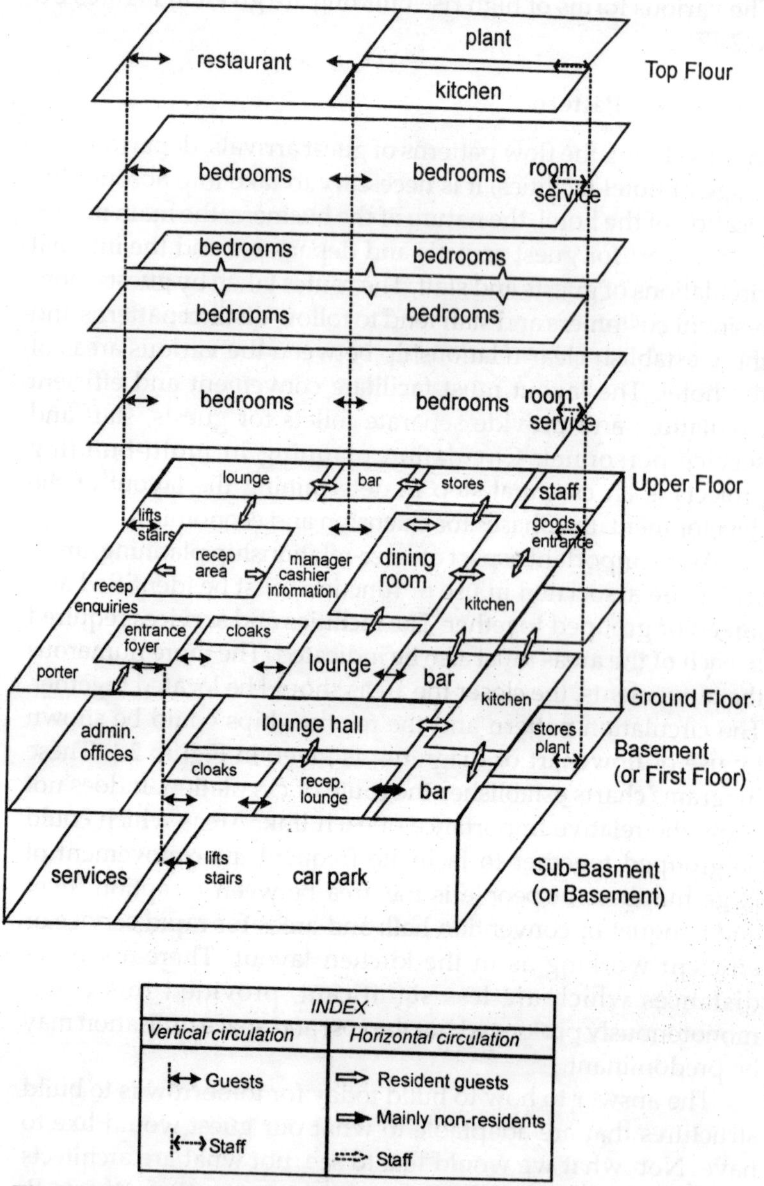

Figure 2.1: A Typical Circulation Pattern (Vertical and Horizontal) for Hotel Guest and Staff.

Modular Construction

This is the most recent and promising development in the construction of hotel buildings. The technique is the answer to the drastic decrease in building costs. This has cut down the construction time and costs by as much as 40 per cent as compared to traditional construction methods.

In this method of construction, room units are constructed separately and hoisted into place by crane. The procedure followed is to place in from all necessary electrical and plumbing conduits along with reinforcing steel, and to pour concrete to form the room module. After curing, the unit is ready to be trucked to the site and placed into position. Thus, the buildings are relatively of low cost, time saving in construction, fire-resistant and virtually sound proof as well.

Slip Forming

This is another recent technique of concrete extension in the hotel construction. The technique was used to raise the exterior walls and some of the interior structure of a 15-story hotel in St. Petersburg, Florida. It enabled the hotel to be 'topped out' in just eight days. In Norfolk, Virginia, the slip forming technique used in construction of a 14-story motor-inn enabled the builders to cut three months from the normal constructions time for a property of this size. In the Norfolk property a three-foot thick reinforced slab was poured for the foundation. Then using a specially constructed wood and steel form, workmen poured concrete into the form continuously at the average rate of 9½ inch per hour. At the same time, the form was raised by a number of electrically operated hydraulic jacks while steel re-inforcing rods were inserted into the concrete.

Tri-arc Design

Many advances are taking place in the configuration of hotel buildings. The idea of tri-arc style was introduced by Travelodge International. The main advantages of this type of designing are:

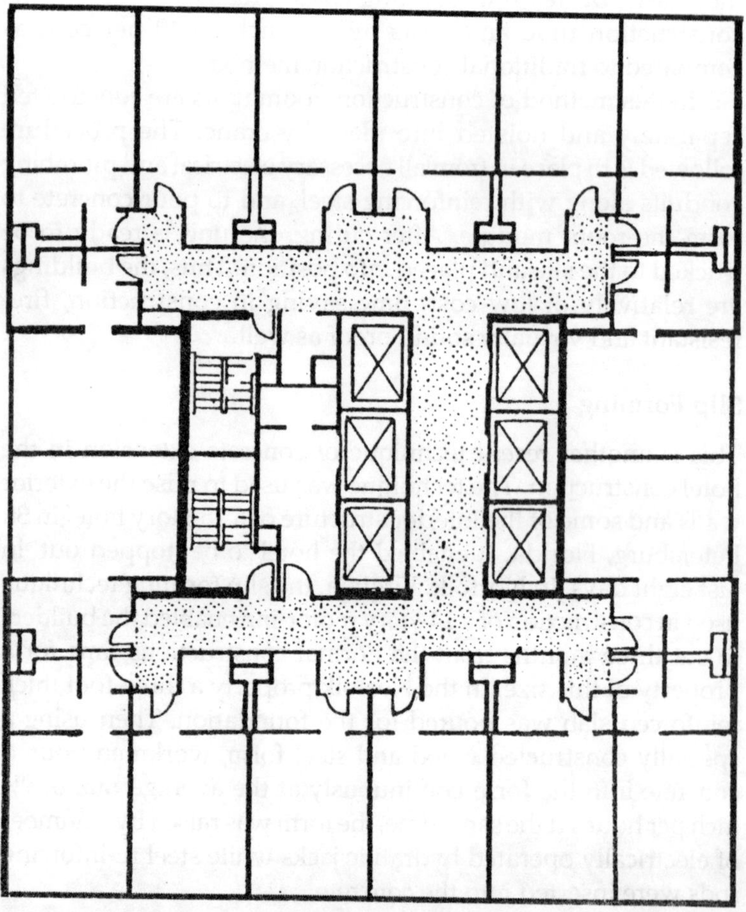

Figures 2.2: A Square Hotel Plan.

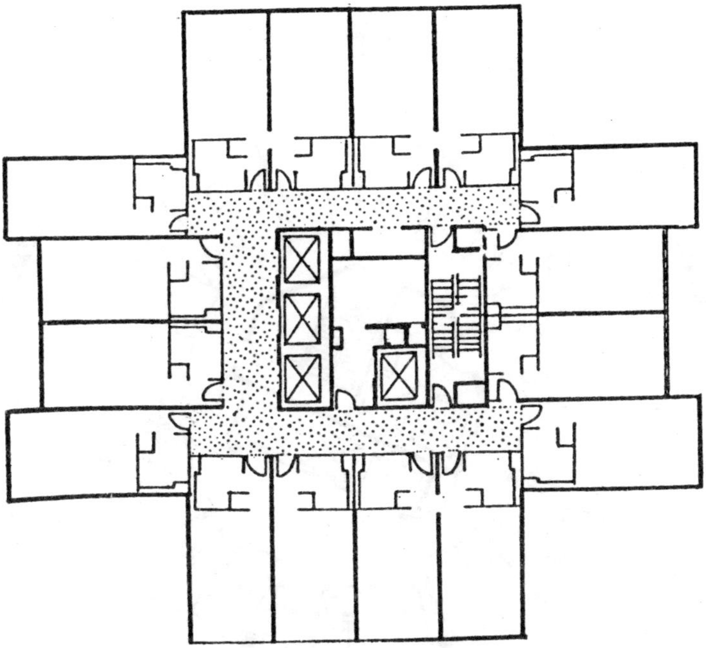

Figure 2.3: A "Deformed" Square Hotel Plan.

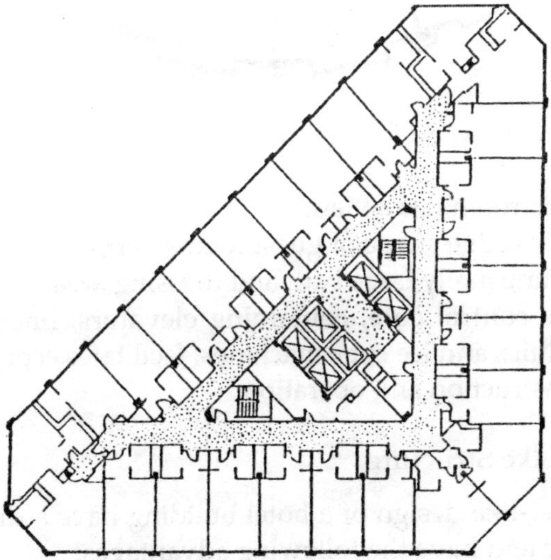

Figure 2.4: A Triangular Hotel Plan with Interior Corridor.

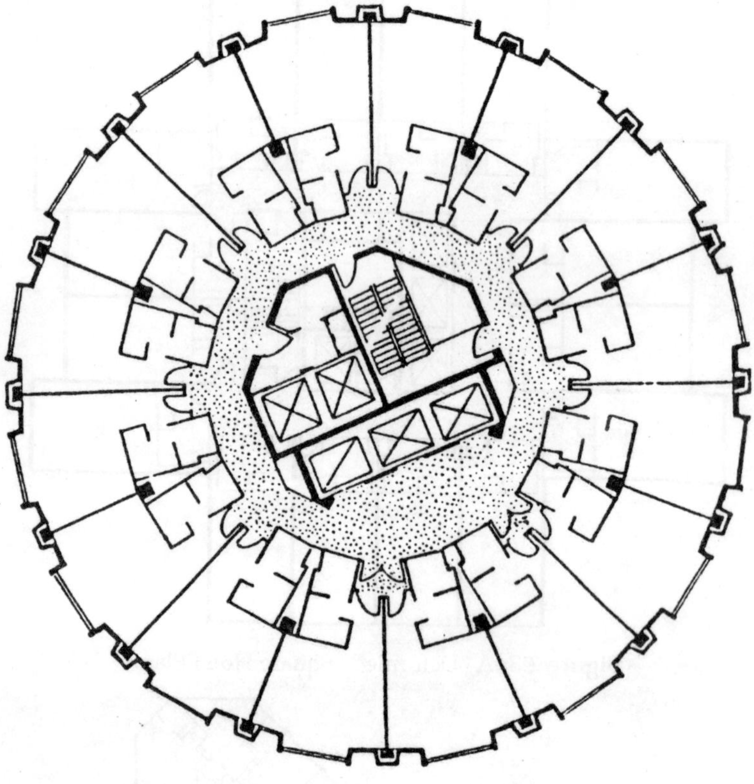

Figure 2.5: A Circular Hotel Plan Stouffer's River-front Towers.

1) Each room has a view.
2) The wedge shape of guest rooms permits each to have an unusually large bath and dressing area.
3) The control core, containing elevators, linen rooms, utilities and ice cube machines, facilitates economies in construction and operation.

Cylinder-Like Structure

The cylinder-like design of a hotel building have a distinctive appearance and have the following advantages:

1) Concentration of service and utility equipment at the centre core.
2) Lower construction and operating costs.
3) All guest rooms on the outer-side with view.
4) Ready-made for the popular roof top revolving restaurant or lounge.
5) Minimum resistance to wind.
6) Suitable for sites where land costs are high and minimum area is available.
7) Compatibility with circumferential ramps leading to parking.

Most of the hotel have been built as horizontal slabs, rectangular shaped buildings. In the beginning they were one or two stories high. Then with the development of structural steel and building expertise hotel shot up into sky. Later hotels took on all sort of shapes. Now we find:

1) Horizontal slabs, rectangular shape,
2) 'L' shaped,
3) 'Y' shaped, and
4) Cylindrical.

The hotel built in rectangular form permits orientation along with an east-west axis so the room face south and north. Such orientation to the room avoids facing the guest room to the west when the heat of the afternoon sun can drive up the cost of air-conditioning in a warm climate. Balconies can be built to project four to six feet from the guest room and provide a partial screen. Vertical walls separating each unit are also helpful in excluding direct sunlight.

Most budget/economy hotels could be built on the barracks plan and if a moderate climate, you can avoid the necessity of inside a hallways, an added cost.

Circular form plan is the most efficient in terms of surface to volume ratio. The guest rooms are necessarily at least partially pie-shaped. The rectangular slab design is more efficient than the more compact, nearly square tower. The corner of a pure square-shaped hotel are often left void because of the difficulty in providing direct corridor access to them the floor plans below show the circular slab, square and a deformed-square floor plan for hotels. To avoid a slab-sided, uninteresting exterior, a hotel that commands a view is likely to have a balcony on each guest room. The balcony adds glamour and architectural interest to the building.

Panel wall construction began in 1950s. Credit for such construction goes to William Tabler for using the first true curtain or panel hotel wall in the Hartford Statler. The curtain wall replaces masonry, in light weighted, and has twice the insulating factor of masonry construction, a factor in reducing air-conditioning requirements. The curtain wall is also more water light than masonry. By using panel walls, the heavy columns needed to support masonry are moved from the outside wall to the interior of the building.

For Statler Hilton in Dallas, Mr. W. Tabler used cantilevered flat slab construction. These slabs are raised along a central core and are held in place by a central support. This reduces the number of column and the size of the foundation by 50 per cent. No beams are required or used, less reinforcing steel needed. Another advantage in the use of the flat slab construction is the need for our half the used number of columns in the lobby. These are columns that usually get in the way and have to be covered with expensive marble.

Planning and Designing of a Hotel

The planning of a hotel project is affected by such factors as size, type and function, financial economies, sitting and operation. Due to the rapid expansion in hotel building, there emerged some uniform design and planning approaches. To achieve improved levels of consumer comfort and of economic and efficiency in hotel operation, hotels are guided by the design consultants. These guidance are relating to three prime functional areas in the hotel:

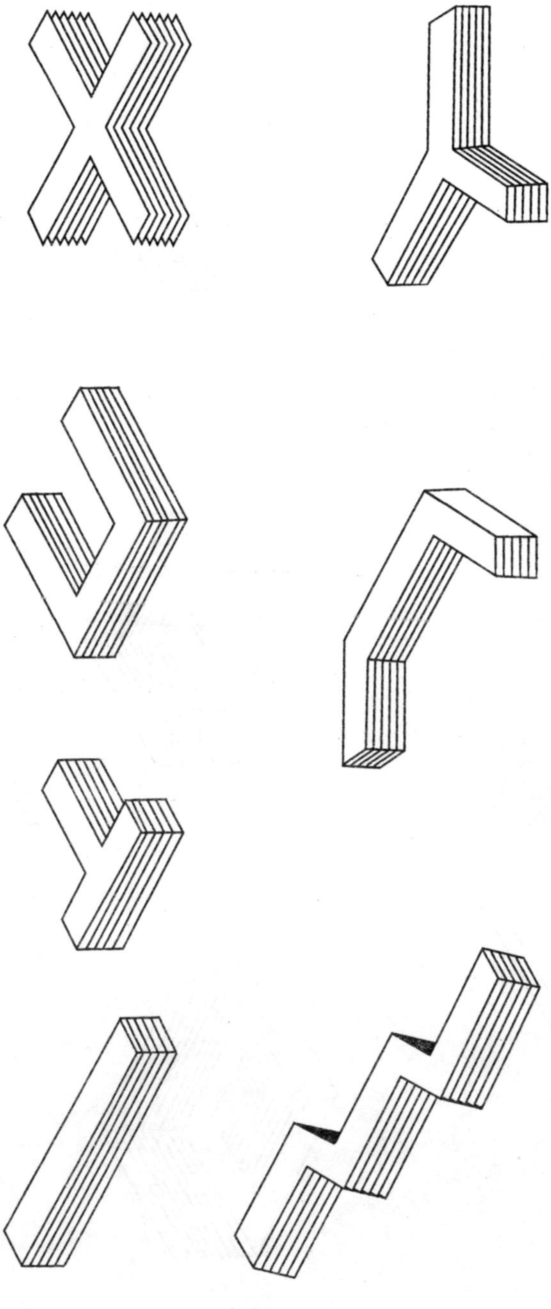

Figure 2.6: Typical Range of Shapes for Hotel Buildings vis-a-vis Hotel Guest Room Blocks—Typical Linear Arrangements of Rooms.

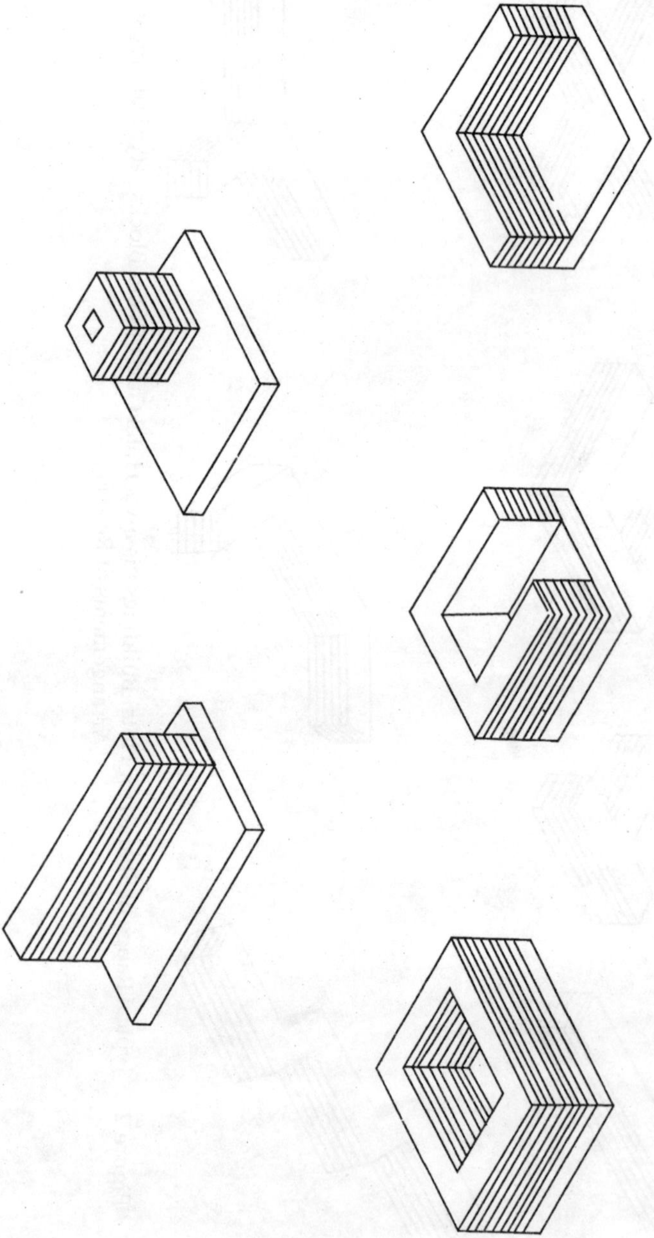

Figure 2.7: Typical Range of Shapes for Hotel Buildings.

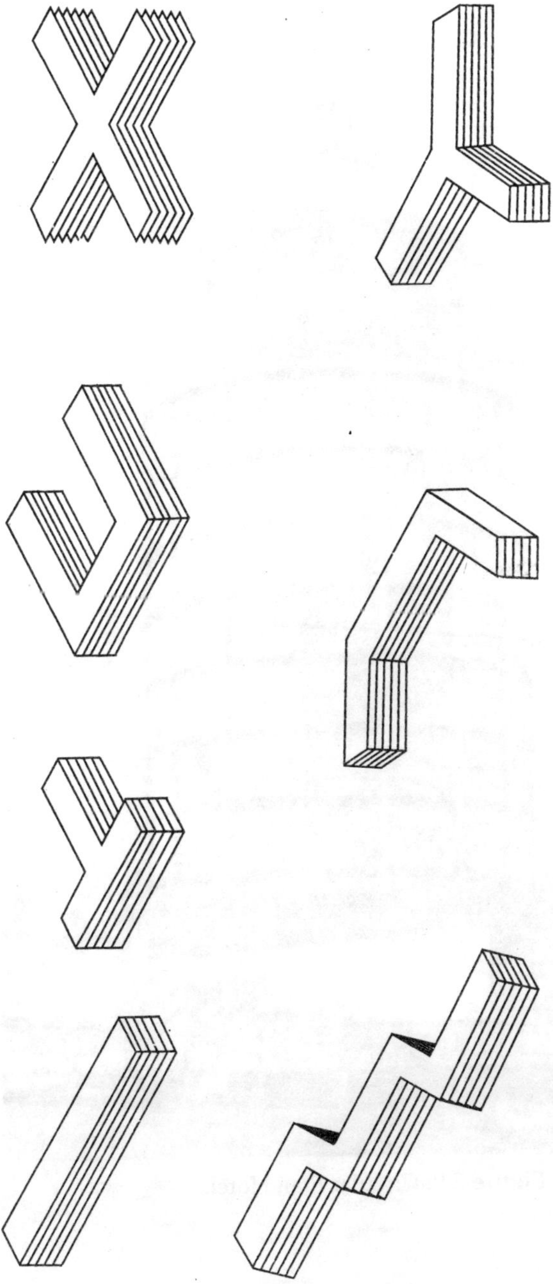

Figure 2.8: Range of Shapes for Hotel Guest Room Blocks.—Typical Linear Arrangements of Rooms.

Figure 2.9: Circular Plan Hotel.

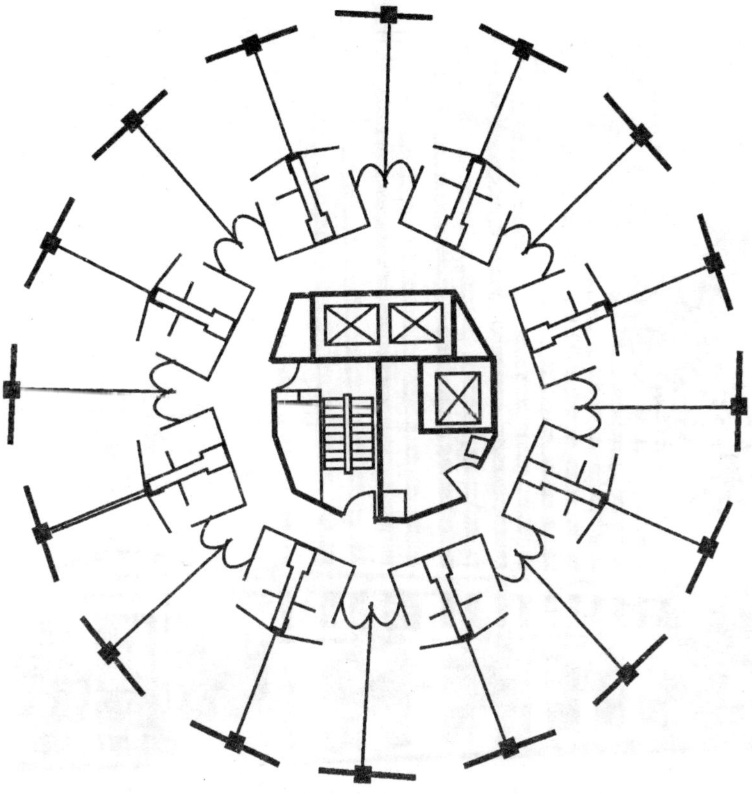

Figure 2.10: Circular Plan for Pattern Building.

Figure 2.11: Slab Shape Hotel Building.

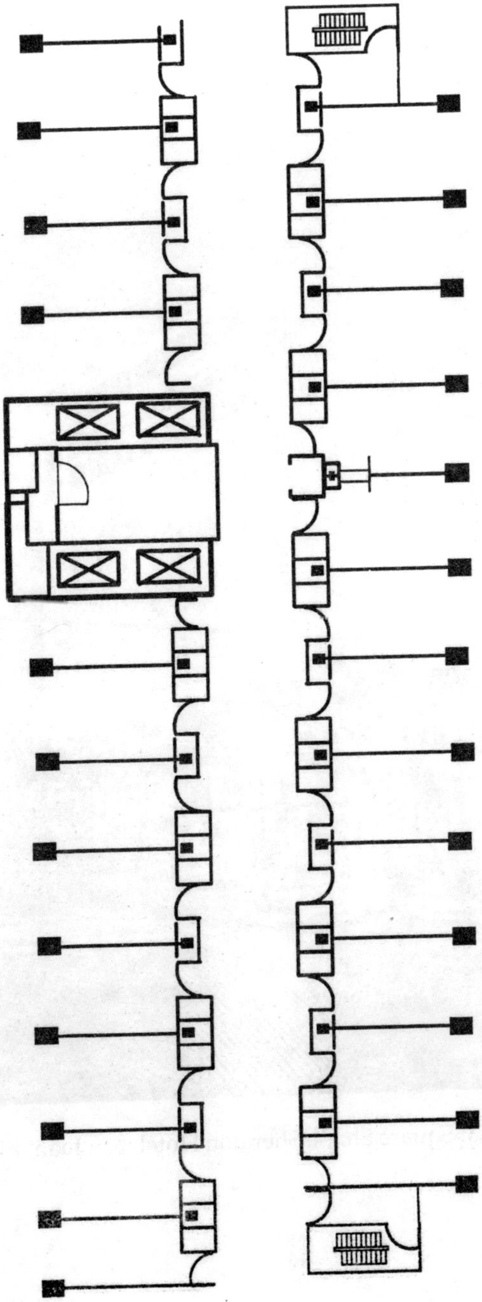

Figure 2.12: Base of a Slab Shape Hotel Building.

Figure 2.13: Square Shape Sheraton Hotel, San Juan, PR.

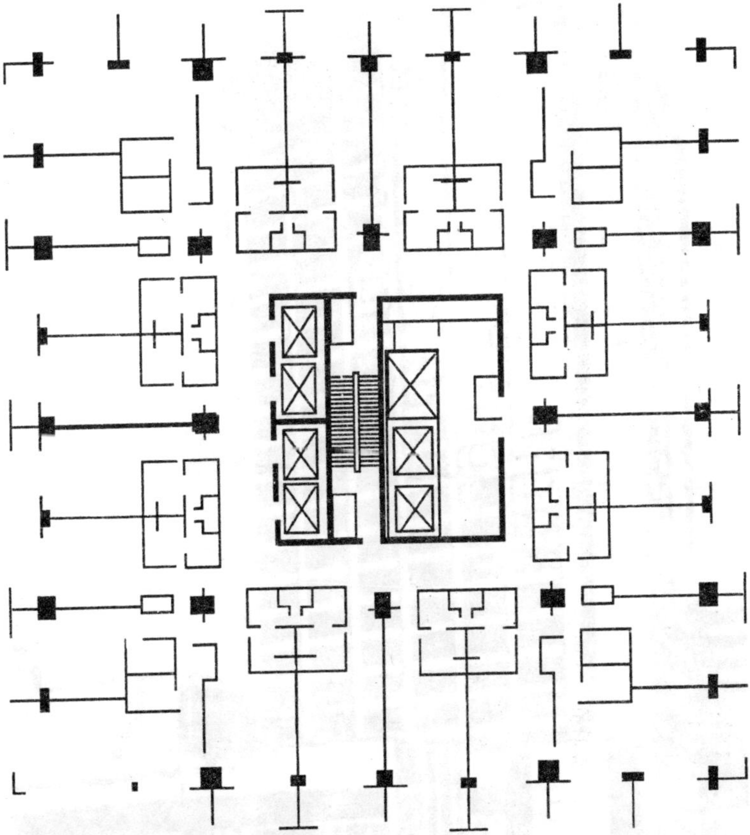

Figure 2.14: Square Shape Hotel Building Plan.

Figure 2.15: Deformed Square: Four Seasons Hotel.

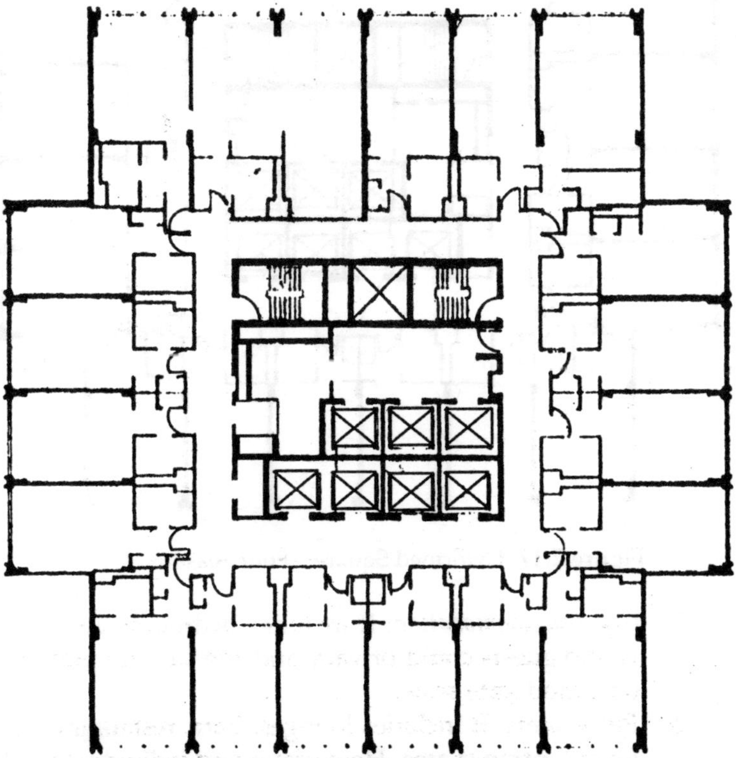

Figure 2.16: Deformed Square Hotel Building Plan.

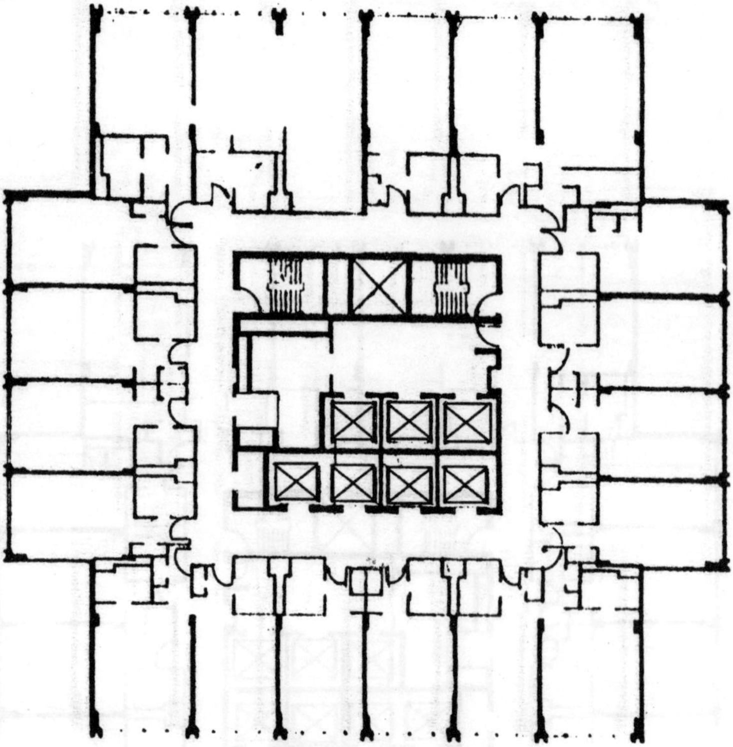

Figure 2.17: Deformed Square—Four Seasons Hotel.

1. *Guest accommodation*: It includes bedrooms and suits, where guests could privacy and services are provided on a moderate scale.
2. *Public areas*: It includes lounges, bars, restaurants and foyer/entrance area. Here group and individual needs are satisfied and privacy is not of vital importance.
3. *Service and administration areas*: It include offices, kitchens and store rooms.

Physical separation of these areas is not essential. Some service functions such as the receipts of goods, food production, beverage, handling and other noisy activities are best located away from guest areas, particularly bedrooms. Other service functions, such as reception work, waiting at table and room service must be closely associated with the public and guest room areas. Figure 2.18 indicates the various functional areas and their relationship.

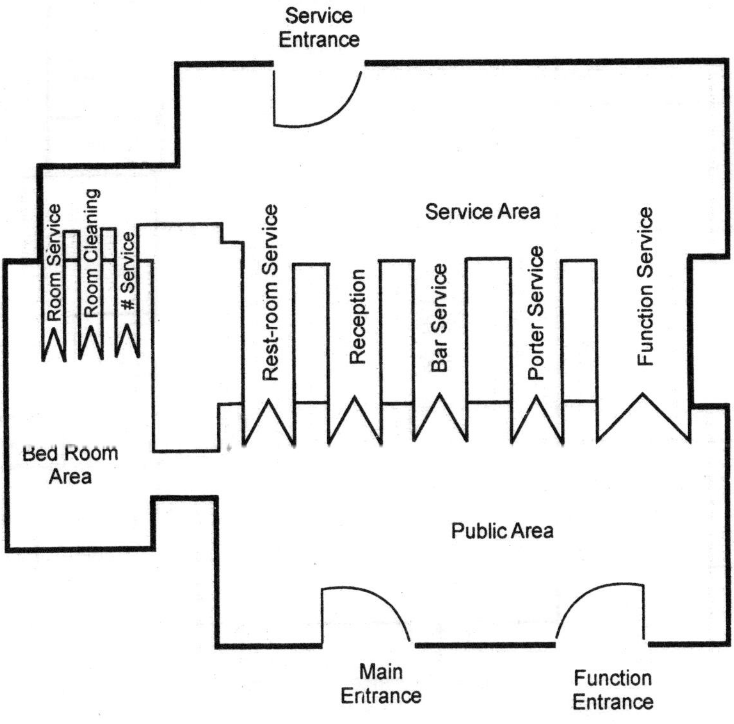

Figure 2.18: Functional Areas and their Relationship.

Figure 2.19 shows the planning concepts of public areas in a hotel.

Planning and Designing of Public Areas

The foyer/lobby is the focal point within the hotel. This area may be multi-purpose, providing space for guest circulation, the reception of incoming visitors, baggage handling and other porterage services, lifts, telephones, cloakrooms and toilets, office accommodation, shop concessions and lounge facilities.

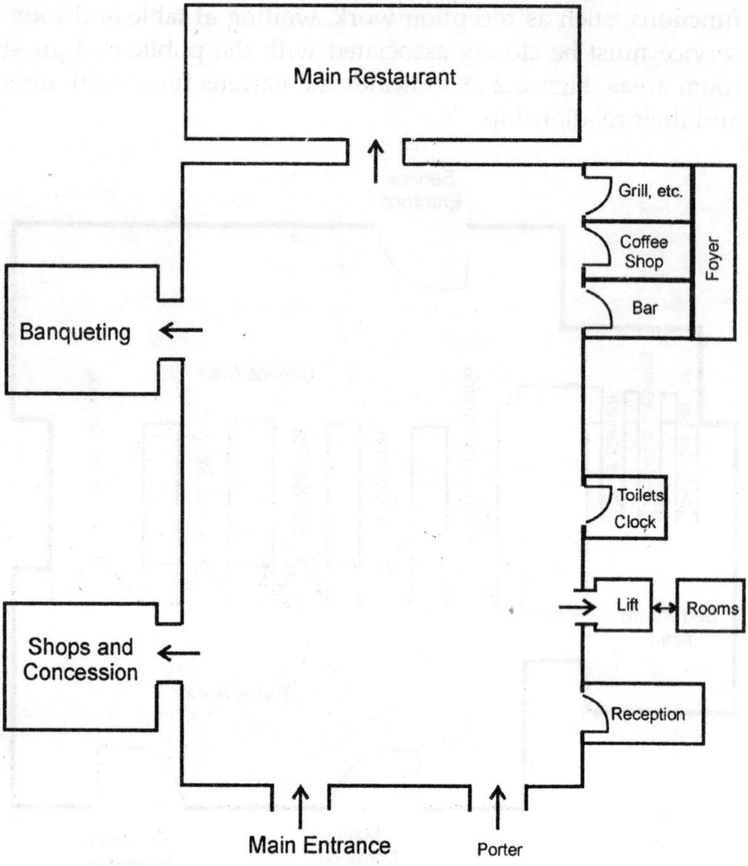

Figure 2.19: The Planning Concepts of Public Areas in a Hotel.

It also give access to bars, grill rooms, restaurant and other catering areas and acts as a buffer between these sales areas and the main entrance at times of peak usage. Separate access to coffee shop, bar and to banqueting suites is desirable so that non-resident hotel users can be segregated from resident guests. This prevents overloading the main hotel services, such as cloak-room and toilet accommodation. Separate facilities should be provided adjoining each subsidiary entrance. At an early stage in the design programme, provision of disabled guests should be considered. This involves access ramps at the main entrance and special features in toilets and other areas designed to cater for those confined to a wheelchair. The relationship between functional areas depends on site economies and planning restrictions. The modern travel is to find bedrooms areas housed either in a separate building away from the public and service areas or in a lower slab built over a lower podium containing the public rooms. In the later concept, mostly in city centre development, the main door located at street level is potentially the most valuable. It can be planned for guest reception, bars, coffee shops, grill bar and other highly profitable operations.

These three main functional areas require detailed planning and careful thought for the layout of the building. Particular consideration should be given to the following to achieve the objectives:

1. *Design*: The design of a hotel should be such as it could function efficiently, smoothly, with economy of labour and on strictly on commercial lines.
2. *Environment*: It must create a pleasant environment for all hotel users—guests, staff, maintenance personnel and outside contractors.
3. *Flow Areas*: There should be a provision of readily discernible flow areas throughout the hotel, not only for all hotel users, but also for food stuffs and all main services.
4. *Ease*: Ease of building, services and house-keeping maintenance.

Hotels have been among the first public buildings to introduce the latest in the facilities. Most of the hotel built before the twentieth century were likely to be block structures. The unimaginative block design has continued to the present day. The large hotels of the twentieth century are in America are towns in themselves. The Dallas Slater Hilton Hotel has a capacity of 10,000 people, the Palmer House 15,000 and the Conrad Hilton 20,000. The telephone switchboard in the Conrad Hilton has more equipment than is used in a city with a 35,000 population.

According to William B. Tabler, architect, for many Hilton Hotels, it takes from two to five years, sometimes even seven years, to put together a large hotel. There is the matter of land acquisition, architectural planning, financing and finally the construction of the building. Actually planning for the guest rooms is only a minor part of the designing a hotel; planning the dinning facilities is a particular challenge and calls for an experienced food service consultant to layout the kitchen equipment. Night clubs and ballrooms, shops, offices, telephone rooms, refrigeration, incineration and boiler plants are part of the hotel. Some of the large hotels may have medical department with emergency rooms, isolation rooms and laboratories.

There is a trend to relocate dining room spaces and especially coffee shops so they have direct access to the street. The formal dining rooms are gradually out, and speciality rooms are in. The speciality room almost always is built with access to the street, since patronage from the hotel guest alone will not make it profitable. The cost of transforming dining rooms or other spaces into speciality rooms can be remarkably high. Usually a remodelled dining room requires about six months to a year of operation before it begins to be profitable.

A number of studies to establish criteria for the allocation of space in a hotel, made by the Sonesta Hotel Management revealed the following:

1) In food service areas they allocate 18 to 20 sq. ft. per seat in a dining room. 15 sq. ft. per seat in a coffee shop, 12 to 15 sq. ft. per seat in lounges and bars and 10 to 12 sq. ft per seat in banquet facilities. These figures shows 25 to 33 per cent of the space for free circulation of service personnels within the facility.
2) The kitchen serving, a dining room and a coffee shop should be about 60 per cent of the total area of the dining room and the coffee shop. This indicates that about 10 to 11 per cent sq. ft. should be allowed per seat in these food service areas. If there is a coffee shop only, the kitchen should be about 45 per cent of the size of the coffee shop serving area, allowing 6.75 sq. ft. per seat. Space allowed for food and beverages should be about half that set aside for the kitchen, or about 5 sq. ft. per seat.

3) Banquet kitchen of course are much smaller, only about one-fifth of the space of the banquet facility is needed for the banquet pantry and only about 8 per cent of the banquet area is needed for banquet storage.
4) Space to be allocated for house-keeping and general storage get smaller per guest room as the hotel gets larger, ranging from 8 sq. ft per guest room in a 1000-room hotel to 15 sq. ft. in a 100 room property. The same relationship is the need for space for administration and rooms department, ranging from 3 ft. per guest room in 1000-room hotel up to 5 ft. per guest room in a 100-room property.
5) The needs of the personnel for eating facilities, lockers, lounge, showers, and so on, requires due consideration. Approximately 7 sq. ft. should be allotted per guest room in a 100-room property for employees facilities.
6) The location of towel racks and hooks is a part of the architect's problem. Towel hooks are placed so that the guest will use a towel an average of three times before throwing it into the hamper. Towel shelves are located so that towel can be reached from the tub and so cuts the laundering of bath mats by half.

The hotel designers must attempt to maximise a 'quality experience' in a minimum of space. Once a desirable room layout has been achieved the room is then replicated tens and even hundreds of times in the same hotel or in a chain of properties. The savings in itmes of rupee may be considerable. Guest rooms tend to run to a standard of about twelve feet wide and twenty-four to twenty-six feet long, including the bath room. Some of the hotel designers tend to make suits two or three times larger and often plan them for two levels connecting by a stairway.

To save space, many hotels have introduced combination sofa heads, in some cases the old Murphy Bed, which folded up into a wall space, has reappeared.

Special attention should be devoted to the design and furnishings of a guest room, since a guest room is repeated several hundred times in a large hotel. Savings in space or cost of furnishing is also repeated. For a time, bedrooms got smaller and smaller but the trend now is toward larger and more comfortable bedrooms. The use of double panel has permitted "glass-walls" to be part of the building. The silent and heat-resistant glass muffles up to 66 per cent more of the transmitted noise than plate glass. The sound ways are converted into heat energy by absorption into a treated inner layer between the double glazing. A self-shaded glass eliminates glare and heat.

In 1977, the Sheraton Corporation introduced a room plan that can be used in almost any room which, with the addition of a draw curtain and a sofa bed, changes the typical bedroom into a combination bedroom/sitting room.

The new convention hotels usually include an assembly room, a banquet room, smaller meeting and private dining rooms, a registration lobby, and an exhibition hall. Dining rooms and meeting rooms should be near and on the same level as kitchen, if possible for reduction in wage costs. A hotel built as a 'Y' shape with three wings emanating from a central core which houses the kitchen.

Space Allotment

The Sonesta Hotel's management has done a number of studies to establish criteria for the allocation of space in a hotel.

S. No.	*Area*	*Space Allocation*
1.	Food service in dining room	18 to 20 sq. ft per seat
2.	Coffee shop	15 sq. ft. per seat
3.	Lounges and bars	12 to 15 sq. ft. per seat
4.	Banquet facilities	10 to 12 sq. ft.

These features allow 25 to 35 per cent of the space for free circulation of service personnel within the facility.

These studies indicate that the kitchen serving a dining room and coffee shop should be about 60 per cent of the total area of the dining room and the coffee shop. This indicate that about 10 to 11 sq. ft. should be allowed per seat in these service areas. If there is a coffee shop only, the kitchen should be about 45 per cent of the size of the coffee shop serving area, allowing 6¾ sq. ft. per seat. Space allowed for food and beverage storage should be about half that set aside for the kitchen, or about 5 sq. ft. per seat.

Banquet kitchens, of course, are much smaller, only about one-fifth of the space of the banquet facility is needed to the banquet pantry and only about 8 per cent of the banquet area is needed for banquet storage.

Space to be allocated for house-keeping and general storage gets smaller per guest room as the hotel gets larger, ranging from 8 sq. ft. per guest room in a 1000-room hotel to 15 sq. ft. in a 100-room property. The same relationship is seen in the need for space for administration and some department, ranging from 3 ft. per guest room in a 1000-room hotel up to 5 ft. per guest room in a 100-room property.

Often overlooked in planning hotels are the needs of the personnel for eating facilities, lockers, lounge, showers and soon. Approximately 7 sq. ft. should be allotted per guest room in a 100-room property for employees facilities.

The allocation of towel racks and hooks is a part of the architect's problem. Towel hooks are placed so that the guest will use a towel an average of three times before throwing it into the hamper.

The most critical parameter of the success and cost of a hotel project is the guest satisfaction. Most other buildings need not be nearly as sensitive to guest comfort as a hotel.

A hotel project is developed through the combined efforts of the architect and engineer, the developer/owner, technical consultants and future operating personnel. The developer/owner has a long-term capital interest in a project. The development division provides technical assistance and design review from the conceptual development through construction. This division is retained as a planning consultant who have no corporate management responsibility. The technical assistance personnel should also be concerned about the costs.

The hotel has many characteristics that make it different from the conventional commercial office or apartment building. Some of the operating requirements of the hotel that call for specific design responses are:

1) Daily Schedule

Hotels are open to the general public 24 hours per day, 365 days a year. There is a cyclical regularity to the schedule, individual meetings and functions, varying room occupancies, weekend and seasonal adjustments.

2) Functional Elements

Hotels include a combination of disparate spaces with very different characteristics, mechanical and electrical requirements, degrees of compartmental, freedom of access, and so on.

3) Guest Services

The required services which the hotel provides includes: maid, valet, laundry, luggage and food sources are provided to room guests, some of them on 24 hour bases, snack, meal, banquet and beverage service is provided in coffee shops, various dining rooms, function halls, bars and lounges and areas adjacent to recreational spaces on an 18—24 hour basis.

Beverage service is frequently found in hotel lobbies. Individual meeting rooms, exhibit areas/books, audio-visual equipment, close circuit TV, stenographers, and so on are provided for conventions.

Swimming pools, health clubs, and game rooms are now common in city hotels, golf, tennis and other land-based recreational activities are provided, maintained and staffed at resorts. In addition, many hotels have provided direct dial telephone, in-room movies, automatic wake-up, electronic room security, computerised reservation and billing, and room status system.

Energy management has become one of the most important control aspect in hotel business and involves the design of the hotel building. It also involves the designing of less glass area, the use of solar screens (screens to shut out the sun when not wanted), increased insulation, consideration of building the hotel into the ground with clerestory windows to let the light into a central well or patio, with guest room facing the well.

Equipment is purchased with particular consideration for the life cycle. Controls are installed which permit energy reduction during the peak load hours. For example, ice machines can be purchased that will not be operated during the period when there is peak load demand on electricity. No hot water need to be heated during that period either, instead it can be stored from times when energy cost is less.

The use of solar collectors to collect heat from the sun and use it in heating the water for the hotel. Several hotels, especially resort hotels, could add collectors which permit a large impact of energy (BTU's) from the sun and a reduction in the amount of oil consumed. Several hotels are using solar energy to heat water up to 140°F and some are using solar energy for air-conditioning. The collectors track the sun across the sky and concentrate and focus the rays on copper absorption tubes. Water in the tube is heated almost to steam and is then pumped to absorption chillers of an air-conditioning system. Most hotel are installing solar collector panels on the roof aimed at the sun so as to get a maximum sun shine each day. The heated water can be used in the kitchen or can be pumped by tubes to guest rooms where blowers transfer the heat from the tubes into the room for heating.

Some hotels are designed with a specific market in mind such as:

1) The upper income group,
2) The travelling men,
3) The conventioneers,
4) The corporate training group,
5) The air-traveller etc.

The highway hotel is appealing to all possible markets, anyone with the price and the inclination to stop at the hotel. The highway traveller is almost anyone with a car, although he may be a tourist on a travelling men. A motel located in an industrial park area has probably identified its market a being largely people who have business at the park. A resort hotel, located some distance from the market, must be much more highly selective in its clientele and must design the hotel appropriate to that market.

Another problem is the automobile parking for hotels. Many hotels succeeded or failed depending upon parking availability. The Christopher Inn of Columbus, one of the most attractive, produced a novel approach to the parking problem. The first three floors of the circular inn are a ramp upon which cars can be parked. The inn begins on the fourth floor and extends up ten stories. All guest rooms have a view since they are on the outside of the circle. The rooms necessarily must be scmewhat pie-shaped. The parking requirements in a hotel could be stated as follows (Podd and Lesure 'Planning and Operating Motels and Motor Hotels').

1) One parking space for each guest unit.
2) One parking space for each restaurant seat.
3) One parking space for every three employees.
4) Two additional parking space for service trucks.
5) One unobstructed loading space.

An automobile requires between 300-400 sq. ft. of space, including the drive way but not including the entrance way. It can be seen that parking requirements add up fast as guest room increase. Most of the older hotels have no provision for parking, most of them have to make arrangements with parking garages to handle guest automobiles. Sheraton hotels have instituted a policy of providing free parking for all guests at their hotels, regardless of cost to the hotel.

Recently spectacular in hotel design has been created. A number of new hotels have departed radically from the traditionally designed hotels which better fit the character of a particular location. Instead of being built by hotelmen as in the past, the new properties are being built almost extensively by developers. In 1967, the Regency Hyatt Hotel in Atlanta with its twenty-one storey open lobby or 'atrium' established a new trend in hotel architecture. It placed a series of similar huge-lobbied hotels. The San Francisco Hyatt with its preventive storey lobby seems to fit San Francisco, an airy city built in hills.

The Century Plaza Hotel in Los Angeles, was also a landmark in hotel construction in that it created its own environment by including a handsome garden, which the lobby overlooks. Its garden restaurant, glass-walled on the garden side, contributes to the garden ambience.

Since the opening of the Atlanta Hyatt Regency, John Potmana, who designed that spectacular hotel, has had the greatest impact on hotel design of any architect. The Regency concept are rooms surrounding an open lobby, the scale, the grandeur, the multi-storied mobiles, glass-sided elevators gliding up and down the lobby, in full view to those in the lobby and elevators. The open lobbies, soaring to the top of the hotel are called atrium's from the Roman Patios of the same name. The lobbies are an exposition of space, an attempt to overcome the tight and cramped space of the central city. Forty foot trees, lakes, open restaurants, water falls, 'people space'—elevators and people moving on different balcony levels—give the atrium a linear kinetic, quality. Birds, trees, reflecting pods, vines, trailing down from guest room balconies within the atrieum, grounded and hanging sculptures add interest and warmth. The lobbies are not only filled with guests of the hotels but have become tourist attractions in their own right.

Chapter 3

Standard Space for Accommodation

Planning and designing of space requires due consideration. It determines the profitability of the hotel and restaurant business. A careful plan consideration to this aspect will benefit the hotel throughout its business operations. Some guidelines are given in Table 3.1 to prospective hoteliers and restauranters to enable them for an ideal space management and organisation.

Minimum standards for hotels and guest houses, including hotels and inns, were also drawn up by the British Tourist Authority, the English Tourist Board, the Scottish Tourist Board and the Wales Tourist Board. The BTA regards adherence to the minimum standards as a basic criterion for the inclusion of establishments in its publications. Some of these standards are given in Table 3.2.

These minimum standards are applicable for accommodation in all licensed establishments and all other establishments with four or more letting bedrooms.

1) All bedrooms must have reasonable free space for movement and for easy access to doors, drawers and beds.
2) All beds, other than those used by children, must conform to, or exceed, the following minimum dimensions:

   (*a*) Single beds : 183 cm × 76 cm (6 ft × 2 ft 6 in)
   (*b*) Double beds : 183 cm × 122 cm (6 ft × 4 ft)

Table 3.1: Standard for Hotel Space Management
Area Requirement

	Minimum Sq ft/m²	*Standard Sq ft/m²*	*Luxury Sq ft/m²*
Bedrooms (including lobby and bath):			
Single	60 / 5.5	70 / 6.5	—
Double	90 / 8.5	128 / 12.2	—
Twin	110 / 10.2	215 / 20.0	260 / 24.0
Bath rooms (if calculated separately)	43 / 4.0		
Food and Beverage Areas:			
Kitchen area	25-30% restaurant area		
Restaurant (Luxury)	18 ft² / 1.7 m² per person		
Medium Restaurant	14 ft² / 1.3 m² per person		
Coffee Shop	14 ft² / 1.3 m² per person		
Bar & Lounge	18 ft² / 1.7 m² per person		
Staff Canteen	12 ft² / 1.6 m² per person		
Public Areas			
Banqueting rounds	10—12 ft² (1.11 m²) per person		
Banqueting springs	8—12 ft² (0.93 m²) per person		
Cocktail parties and Receptions	5 ft² (0.46 m²) per person		
Theatre seating	7 ft² (0.65 m²) per person		
Desk seating arrangement	16 ft² (1.49 m²) per person		
Standard of performance as regards to production:			
Coffee Shop server	: 35 covers over lunch period		
	: 25 covers at dinner		
Restaurant silver	: 25 covers at lunch		
Service server	: 15 covers at dinner		
Dishwashers	: 110 cover per hour/per person		
Room attendants	: 12-15 occupied rooms per day per person		
Front office	: 55 occupied rooms per shift per person		

Table 3.2: General Guidelines—Minimum Standards for Accommodation

All bedrooms must conform to, or exceed the following minimum dimensions for floor areas excluding private baths or shower area:

(*i*)	Single bedrooms	5.60 m^2	(60 sq ft)
(*ii*)	Double bedrooms	8.40 m^2	(90 sq ft)
(*iii*)	Twin-bedded rooms	10.20 m^2	(110 sq ft)
(*iv*)	Family rooms:		

Minimum floor area of 280 m^2 (30 sq ft) plus:
5.60 m^2 (60 sq ft) for each double bed and/or
3.70 m^2 (40 sq ft) for each single adult bed, and/or
1.85 m^2 (20 sq ft) for each cot

3) All mattresses must be spring interior, foam or of similar quality, and in sound condition. Bedding must be clean, and in sufficient quantity.
4) Beds must be made daily. Linen must be changed at least once per week and for every new resident guest.
5) All bedrooms must be equipped with a wash basin, having both hot and cold running water, either in the bedroom or in a private bathroom. A mirror must be above, or adjacent to the wash basin.
6) All bedrooms (or bathrooms) must be equipped with an electric shaver point.
7) All bedrooms must be supplied, for every new resident guest, with fresh soap and a clean towel and these must be replenished or changed as required.
8) All bedrooms must be provided with:

(*i*) Dressing table or equivalent, and mirror
(*ii*) Wardrobe, or clothes hanging space, equipped with at least four hangers per person
(*iii*) Adequate drawer space
(*iv*) Bedside table or equivalent
(*v*) One chair, or equivalent, per person (minimum of two in family rooms)
(*vi*) Wastepaper container
(*vii*) Ashtray
(*viii*) One drinking vessel per person (minimum of two in family rooms).

9) All bedrooms must be equipped with bedside rugs or mats, where no carpet is provided.
10) All bedrooms must have at least one window and be adequately ventilated.
11) All bedrooms must be equipped with opaque curtains or blinds on all windows.
12) All bedrooms must be adequately heated, according to season, at no extra charge.
13) All bedrooms must be adequately lit, to the following minimum levels, with a light controlled from the bed:

(*i*)	Single bedrooms	:	110 watts or equivalent
(*ii*)	Other bedrooms	:	150 watts or equivalent

14) All bedrooms must be fitted with a lock that will ensure privacy for guests and security for their property. Guests must be provided with a key to their bedrooms, duplicate or master keys being kept by the management.
15) All resident guests must be allowed access to their bedrooms at all reasonable times.

Bathrooms

1) The establishment must have at least one bathroom, equipped with a bath or shower, for every fifteen resident guests (other than guests in bedrooms with private bathrooms).
2) Hot water must be available at all reasonable times, with no extra charge for baths or showers.
3) All private bathrooms must be equipped with a WC and either a bath or shower.

WCs

1) The establishment must have at least one WC for every ten resident guests (other than guests in bedrooms with private bathrooms).
2) Where there is only one WC, it must not be in a bathroom.

3) All WCs, including those in private bathrooms, must be equipped with toilet paper and a disposal bin.

General

1) The establishment must provide a residents' lounge or lounge area, appropriate to the type of establishment.
2) All public areas must be adequately heated, according to season, at no extra charge.
3) All public areas must be adequately lit for comfort and safety.
4) A telephone must be available for residents' use at all reasonable times.
5) The establishment must be kept clean throughout, and all exterior and interior decorations, furnishings, floor coverings and fittings must be maintained in good condition.

Disabled Guests: Optional Standard

The establishment may or may not be able to accommodate severely disabled guests (e.g. those in wheelchairs). Those that welcome disabled guests, and wish to be so designated in publications, must conform to the following minimum requirements:

1) At least one entrance must either have no steps or be equipped with a ramp whose gradient does not exceed 1 in 12.
2) All doors (including those of WCs, private bathrooms, etc.) must have a clear opening width of at least 74 cm (29 in.) with a head-on approach.
3) All essential accommodation, if not on the ground floor, must be served by an adequately sized lift.
4) Lift gates must be at least 80 cm (31.5 in.) wide; lifts must be at least 122 cm (48 in.) deep and 91 cm (36 in.) wide.
5) At least one bedroom and one public WC must be suitable for disabled guests.

6) In the bedrooms, private or public bathrooms and WCs used by the disabled, the clearance around beds, and to reach wash basins, WCs, etc., must be at least 75 cms (24.5 in.), and there must be turning space of 122 cm (48 in.) by 122 cm (48 in.).
7) The establishment must accept guide dogs, but may exclude them from dining or restaurant areas.
   Although not required as minimum standards, it is strongly recommended that:
   (*i*) All beds, other than those for use by children, conform to, or exceed, the following dimensions:

      Single beds : 190 cm or 6 ft 3 in. × 90 cm or 3 ft.
      Double beds : 190 cm or 6 ft 3 in. × 135 cm or 4 ft 6 in.

   (*ii*) There be at least one bathroom for every ten resident guests (other than those with private bathrooms).
   (*iii*) There be at least one WC for every eight resident guests (other than those with private bathrooms).

Code of Conduct for Tourist Accommodation

There is a code of conduct for establishments providing tourist accommodation and is designed to ensure a fair deal for all guests. In addition to fulfil its statutory obligations, the management undertakes to observe the following code of conduct:

1) To ensure high standards of courtesy, cleanliness, catering, and service appropriate to the type of establishment.
2) To describe fairly to all visitors and prospective visitors the amenities, facilities an services provided by the establishment, whether by advertisement, brochure, word-of-mouth or any other means and to allow visitors to see accommodation, if requested, before booking.
3) To make clear to visitors exactly what is included in all prices quoted for accommodation, meals and

refreshments, including service charges, taxes and other surcharges. Details of cancellation procedures and charges for additional services or facilities available should also be made clear. In the case of establishments with four bedrooms or more, to adhere to the Hotel Industry Voluntary Code of Booking Practice.

4) To adhere to, and not to exceed, prices current at time of occupation, for accommodation or other services.
5) To advise visitors at the time of booking, and subsequent to any change, if the accommodation offered is in an unconnected annexure, or similar, or by boarding out and to indicate the location of such accommodation, and any difference in comfort and amenities from accommodation in the main establishment.
6) To give each visitor, on request, details of payments due, and a receipt, if required.
7) To deal promptly and courteously with all inquiries, requests, reservations, correspondence and complaints from visitors.

Chapter 4

Guest Room Designing

The location and type of guest served is to be considered in designing the type and size of a room in a hotel.

The arrangement of public rooms and service areas, especially when large uninterrupted space are required often conditions the shape and layout the bedroom areas. The following factors affect floor layout:

1) Vertical circulation routes for guests and staff.
2) Emergency stairways.
3) Service lifts for linen, equipment and food.
4) Service ducts for plumbing, electricity and telephone conduits, air-conditioning and ventilation ducts.
5) Service rooms for equipment and linen storage and food preparation.

The number of room on each floor may be governed by special characteristic related to the site and by the layout and dimensions of individual rooms. Furthermore, no bedroom floor plan should be finalised without considering the workload of house-keeping personnel. For example, where a room-maid is capable of serving 12 rooms; the number of rooms assigned to each floor should be in multiples of twelve. Double banking generally afford the most economic floor utilisation, yielding as much as 80 per cent of the total floor space for bedrooms or other revenue producing purposes.

Guest room planning is most important. The reputation of the whole hotel is geared to room design and layout. A guest's decision to revisit a hotel is coloured by his impressions of comfort and walking created by the accommodation.

Figures 4.1, 4.2 and 4.3 are typical floor layout plans for guest rooms.

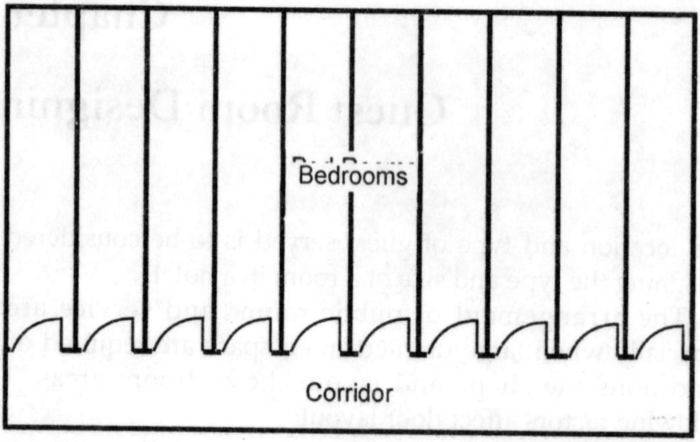

Figure 4.1: Layout Plans for Bedroom Floor—Single Banking.

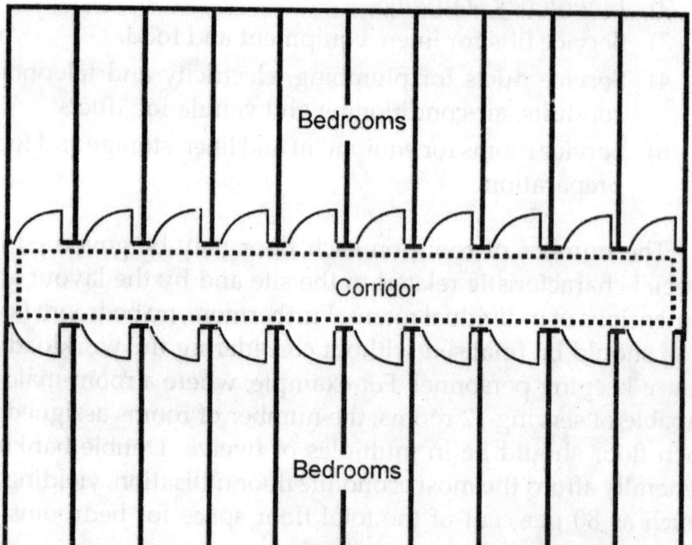

Figure 4.2: Layout Plans for Bedroom—Double Banking.

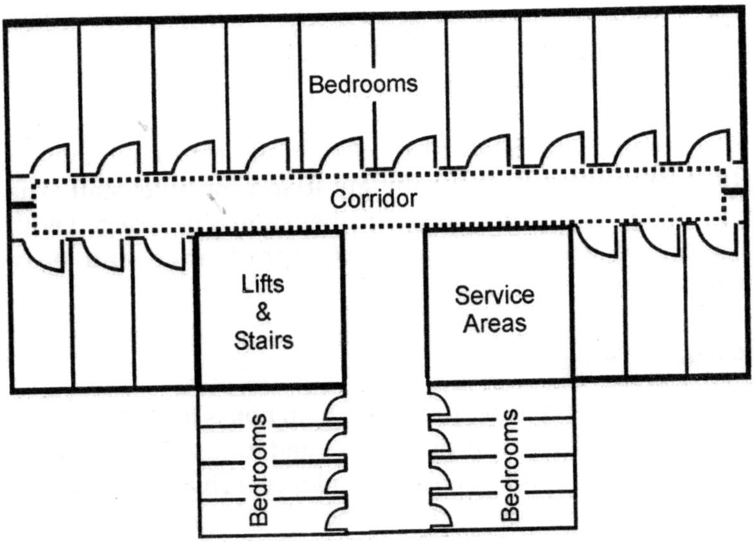

Figure 4.3: Layout Plans for Bedroom—'T' Shaped Arrangement.

A close analysis of the functions of a bedroom is required to have a successful designing. These functions include:

1) *From the Guest Point of View*:

   (*i*) Accommodation for sleeping.
   (*ii*) Accommodation for sitting.
   (*iii*) Accommodation for reading.
   (*iv*) Accommodation for eating.
   (*v*) Accommodation for writing.
   (*vi*) Accommodation for bathing and washing.
   (*vii*) Accommodation for storage of clothes etc.
   (*viii*) Accommodation for storage of travelling cases and bags.

2) *From the Hotel's Point of View*:

   (*i*) Daily bedroom cleaning.
   (*ii*) Periodic or spring cleaning.

(*iii*) Equipment maintenance.

(*iv*) Room decoration.

Planning of the guest rooms should be to achieve an effective solution both for the guest and for hotel staff. The type of furnishings and room finishes should be selected with a view to durability, comfort, appearance and easy maintenance.

Bedroom Design

The modern trend in bedroom design in hotels indicate smaller rental units with identical dimensions and furnishings but a high degree of guest comfort and convenience. Private bathroom is attached to each room and the whole is designed to combine economies of construction fitting out and operation, with the demands of discriminating clientele.

Figure 4.4 is a typical development in design of a hotel bedroom. Decisions affecting the relationship of areas within room (*a*) will be influenced by the positioning of bedrooms in the hotel plan as a whole. The problems of providing an extensive range of services to every bathroom throughout on hotel, forces these areas to be paired alongside a common duct.

Internal sitting, in (*b*) produces problems of mechanical ventilation and artificial illumination. This arrangement allows access to service ducts from the corridor outside each room. It also permits outside walls to be fully exploited, especially where an attractive vista can be made a selling feature for the hotel.

The main structured elements used in tall bedroom block construction should be designed with room sizes in mind. It is common to find the bay size (that is the space between each of the main support posts) large enough for sub-division into two guest room units of equal or unequal size. In such cases, bathroom sizes remain constant and a partition wall determinesindividual room size. In smaller developments, cross

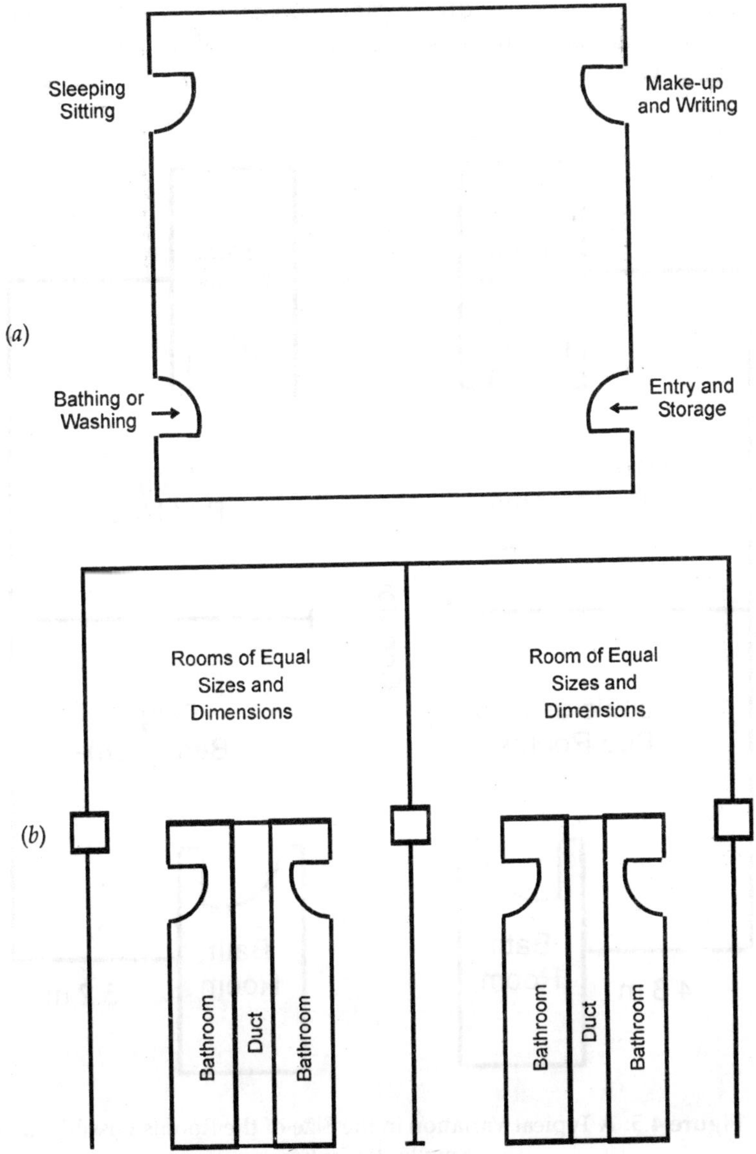

Figure 4.4: A Typical Basic Design for a Hotel Bedroom.

wall construction permits a similar flexibility in room sizes. Alternatively, room widths remain constant and sizes can be varied by adjusting the position of the external wall as given in Figure 4.5.

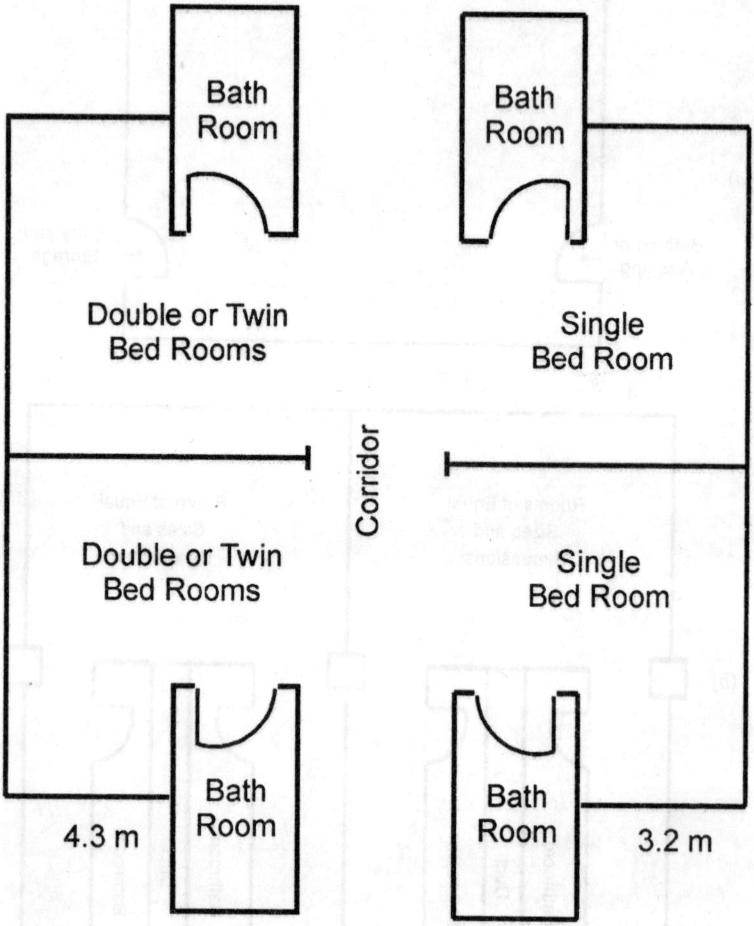

Figure 4.5: A Typical Variation in the Size of the Rooms Possible in Smaller Projects.

Determine the portion of single, studio-type, twin bedded and doubles bedded accommodation in the hotel as a whole. Marketing forecasts may considerably influence this decision. Present trend suggest that, except where it is firmly established that a continuing demand will exist the single accommodation, room are planned to cater for twin-or double bedded occupancy.

The style and type of furnishings, fittings and equipment, should also be taken into account while deciding the design. There are free standing wardrobes and writing tables to streamlined off the floor modular multi-purpose units.

Figure 4.6 shows the interior layout of hotel bedroom which indicates a range of special design features which can be incorporated into room planning.

Figure 4.6: Typical Interior Layout of a Hotel Bedroom.

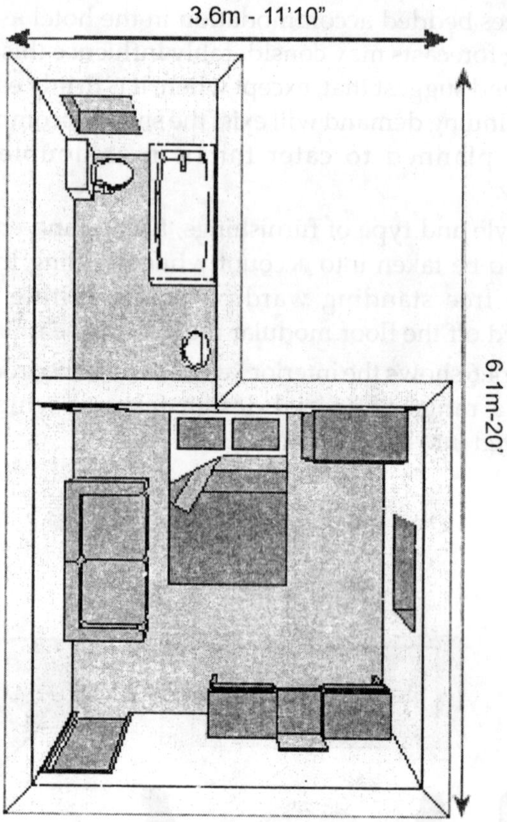

Figure 4.7: Typical Layout of a Bedroom with Bathroom.

Bathroom Planning

A hygienic, almost clinical, approach combining basic equipment such as bath, shower, wash basin and W.C. with a considerable range of ancillary equipment such as paper tissue dispenser, drip-dry rack and telephone should be taken into consideration while designing a bathroom.

Figure 4.8 shows a typical layout of bedroom with private bath. Opposite is a bathroom interior and this highlights the more important design features.

Figure 4.8: Typical Layout of a Private Bathroom.

Guest Room Floors and Framing Systems

Figure 4.9 is a typical floor plan layout of a guest room floor, relating possible room sizes to column framing. By using standard bay width and varying the depths of the front and rear bays, eight different sizes are available. Since a standard bay is held to three-out the guest room floor, room sizes may be varied at will to give desired portions of single, double, twin, studio rooms, etc. per floor. Connecting doors between rooms in each bay gives additional flexibility in accommodation. In the layout shown in the diagram, the end rooms may be rented separately or combined to rent as a suite.

Figure 4.10 has essentially the same variations in room sizes as given diagram in Figure 4.11. Diagram in Figure 4.12, however, is based on cantilevered construction rather than standard framing. Note variation in placement of fire stairs, with increased corridor width and large corner rooms.

Figure 4.11 is less flexible than in diagram given in Figure 4.9 or 4.10. Diagram given in Figure 4.11 uses standard bay widths,

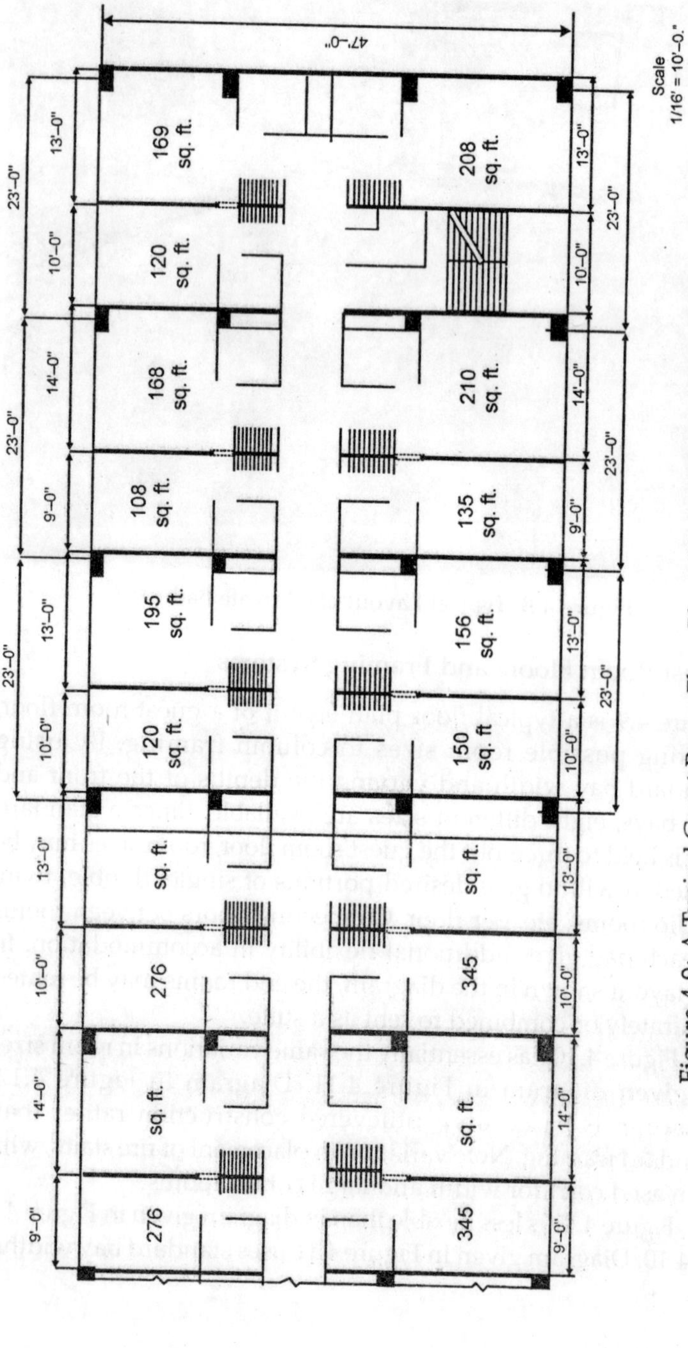

Figure 4.9: A Typical Guest Room Floor Plan—Type 'A' Scale 1/16' = 10'-0."

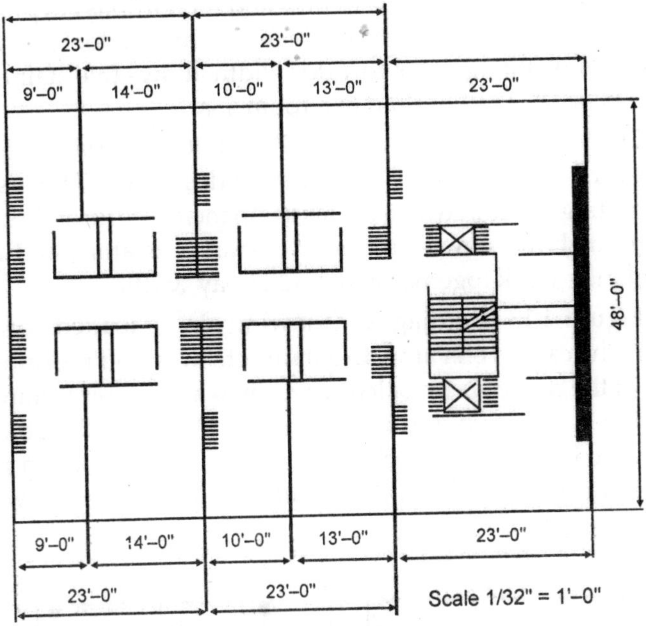

Figure 4.10: Typical Guest Room Floor Plan.

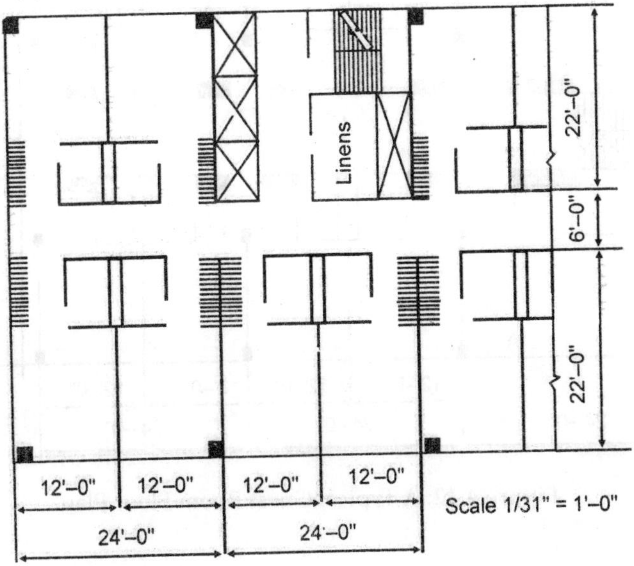

Figure 4.11: Typical Guest Room Floor Plan.

but equal front and rear bay depths and set portions cut possible room sizes to two flexibility is achieved by use of doors between rooms. Note that greater corridor width allows five stair at the end of corridor rather than in a room space.

Diagram given in Figure 4.12 is another variation of the standard bay, double-loaded corridor plan. The use of connecting doors between rooms again increases flexibility. This diagram shows how a case of five stairs, elevators, and lenin room may work together in a double-bay width.

Figure 4.13 is a diagram showing single-loaded corridor plan. The case of elevators fire stairs, etc. work off the opposite side of the corridors (of balcony type in warm-tropical climates) leaving a continuous rows of rooms. Most hotels using the single loaded corridor scheme have little variations in room types and sizes. Balconies and corridors are shown as cantilevered.

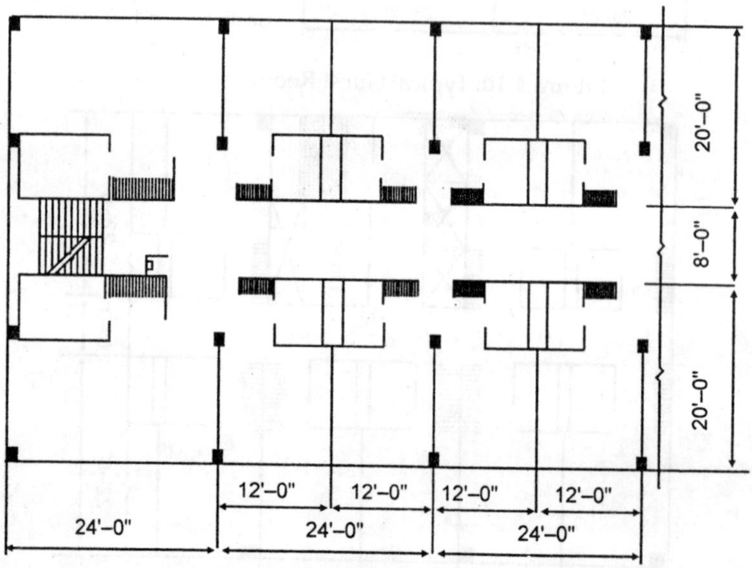

Figure 4.12: A Typical Guest Room Floor Plan.

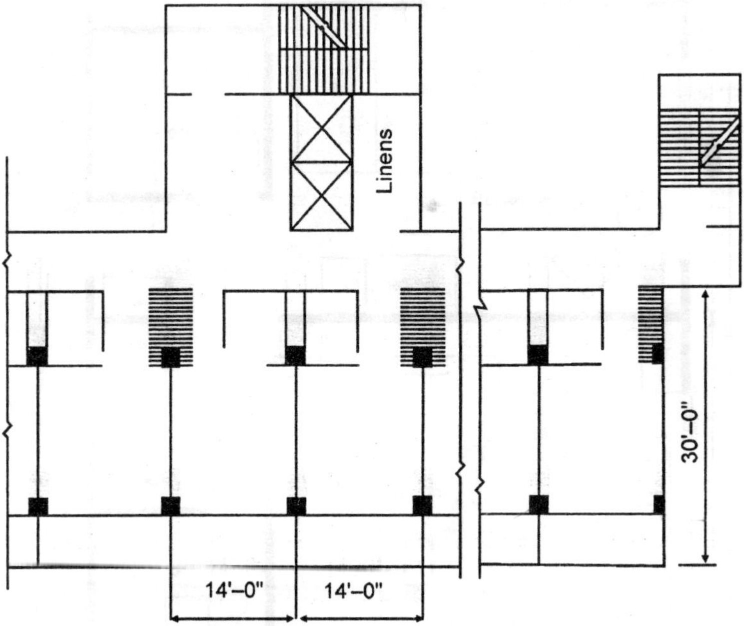

Figure 4.13: A Typical Guest Room Floor Plan.

Guest Rooms Suite Arrangements

Figures 4.14 and 4.15 are diagrams of hotel suits. Two general types are shown with furniture arrangements.

1) *Flexible*: This is luxury room with average or minimum bedroom adjoining units may rent separately.
2) *Apartment*: Living area with kitchenette and one or more adjoining bedroom.

Guest Room Floors Arrangements

Figure 4.14 indicates a typical plan of a guest room floor showing the relationship of rooms, elevators fix stairs and stand pipes. The floor linen and maid's room should contain in addition to clean linen locker facilities, carts and storage for cleaning supplies, laundry, chutes and recommended for solid linens.

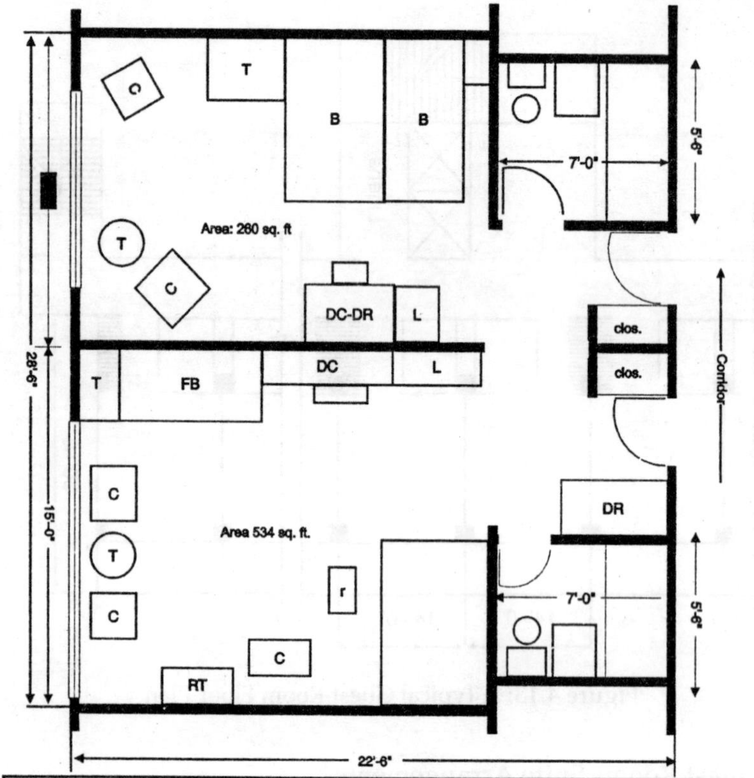

KEY

B = Single Bed, DTC = Dining Table and Chairs, FB = Folding Bed, DC = Desk and Chair, C = Chair, DR = Dresser, T = Table, L = Luggage, RT = Radio-Phonograph or Television.

Figure 4.14: A Typical Flexible Suite.

General regulations of the fire codes which should be kept in mind are:

1) A minimum of two exits is required from each floor elevators not included, without automatic sprinklers, no room should be more than 150 feet from an exit.
2) Fire escapes are not permitted on new buildings.
3) Illuminated signs must be visible from any point in the corridors to main exits or approaches to exits.
4) Each room must have a floor plan showing the exit system.

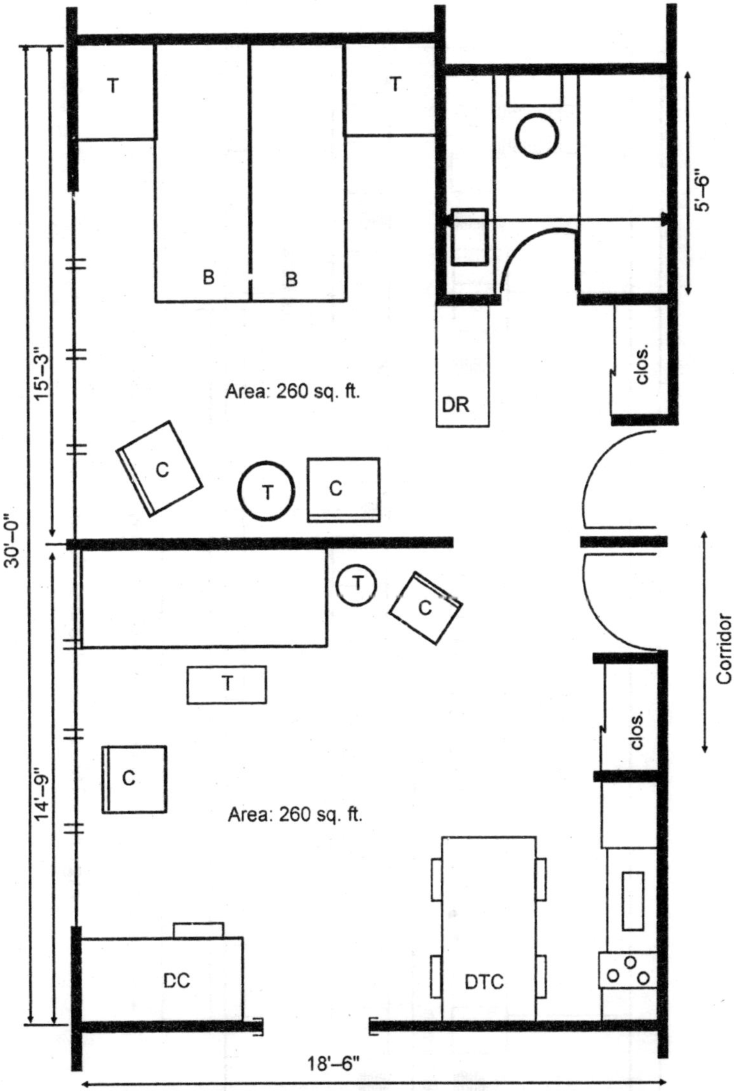

KEY

B = Single Bed, DTC = Dining Table and Chairs, FB = Folding Bed, DC = Desk and Chair,
C = Chair, DR = Dresser, T = Table, L = Luggage,
RT = Radio-Phonograph or Television.

Figure 4.15: A Typical Apartment Suite.

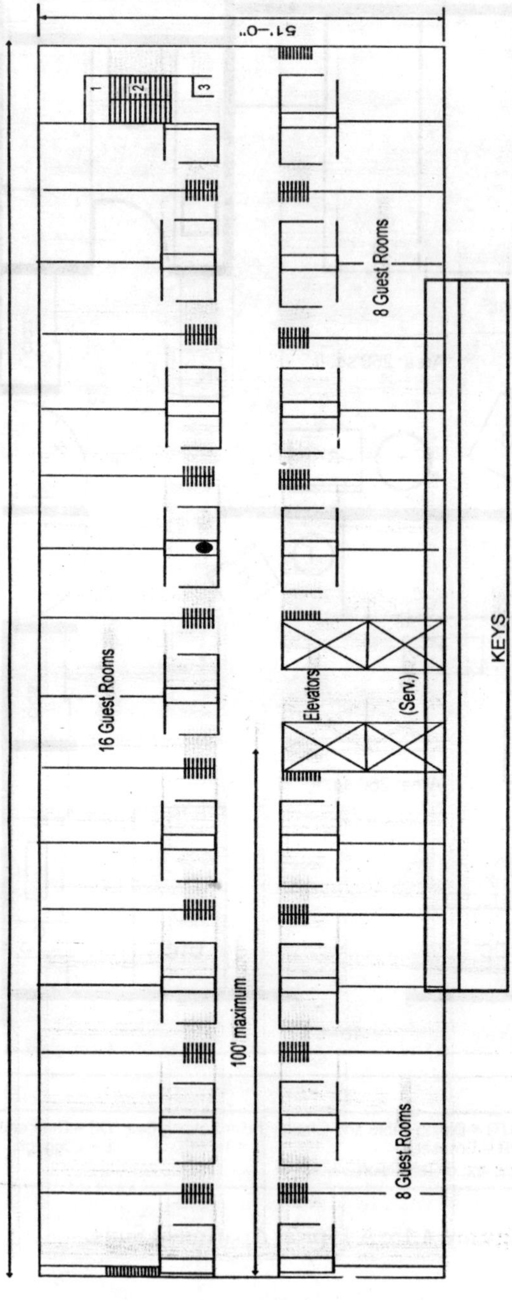

● Stand Pipes, 1. Floor Linen and Maid's Room, 2. Fire Station and 3. Service Sink.

Figure 4.16: A Typical Guest Room Floor.

Guest Rooms Layout with Furniture

Studio type rooms are those which are so arranged and furnished that they function as living room during the day. Where communication doors are desired, the furniture may be rearranged or certain items omitted, to allow sufficient wall space for a door. It may occasionally be desired to set back the entrances to the rooms, particularly when the corridor is narrow and this devices would have a certain additional corridor width.

Figures 4.17, 4.18 and 4.19 show the diagram of typical hotel rooms, with possible furniture arrangement. These diagrams include three basic types of rooms.

1) *Minimum* : Approximately 220 sq. ft. in room.
2) *Average* : Approximately 260 sq. ft. in room.
3) *Luxury or large* : Approximately 330 sq. ft. in area.

Figure 4.20 have rooms with baths on outside wall. Economy and desire to devote available outside wall space to rooms generally predict this arrangement from being used in most transient hotels.

Figure 4.21 calls rooms with balconies. Generally found in resort and transient hotels where main-tropical climate's permit outdoor living. Balconies are shown with three types of rooms, actually may be used with any type.

Key to Furniture: Figures 4.17 to 4.19
B: Single Bed,
C: Chair,
DH: Dresser,
DB: Double Bed,
DC: Desk and Chair,
RT: Radio-phonograph or Television.
FB: Folding Bed,
T: Table,
L: Luggage Rack,

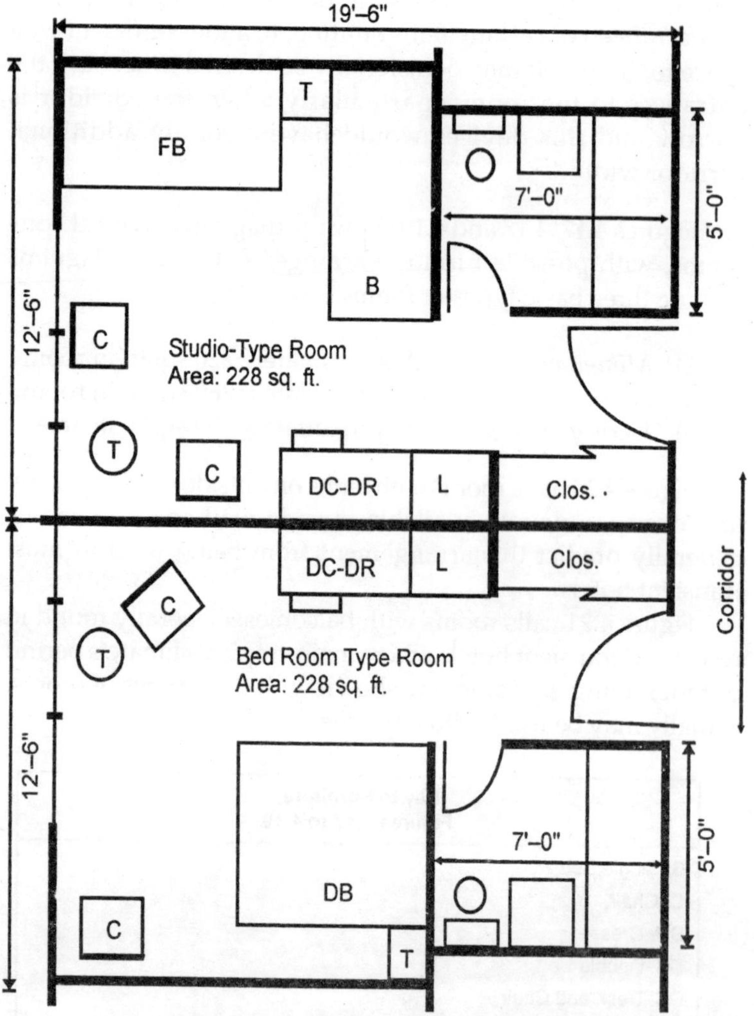

Figure 4.17: A Typical Minimum Room.

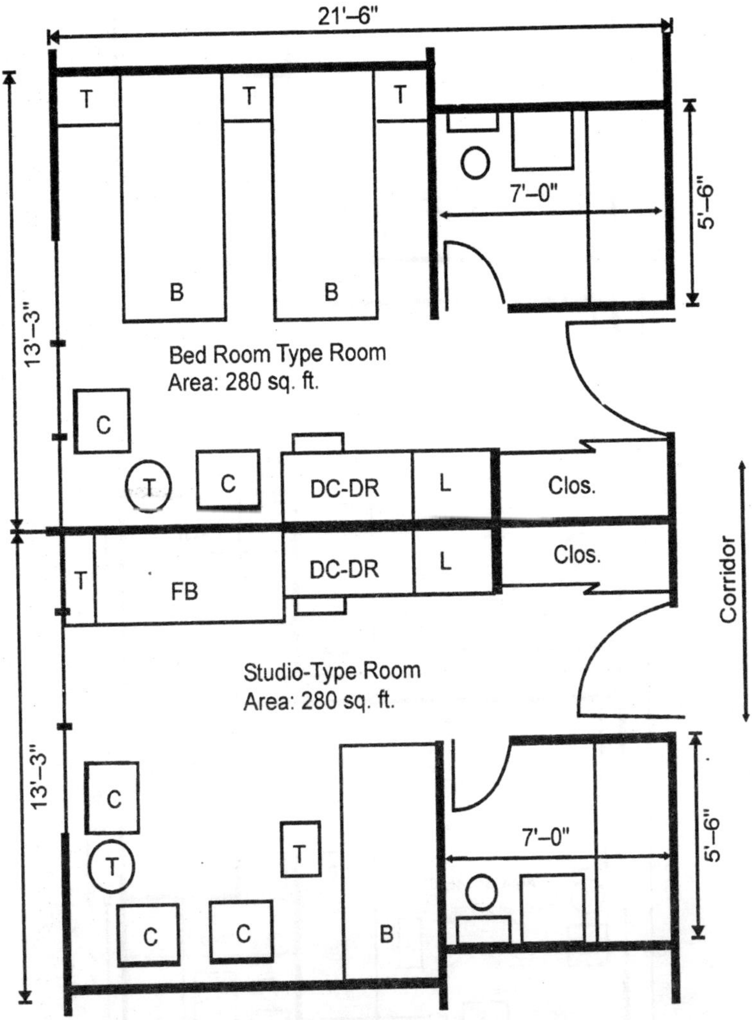

Figure 4.18: A Typical Average Room.

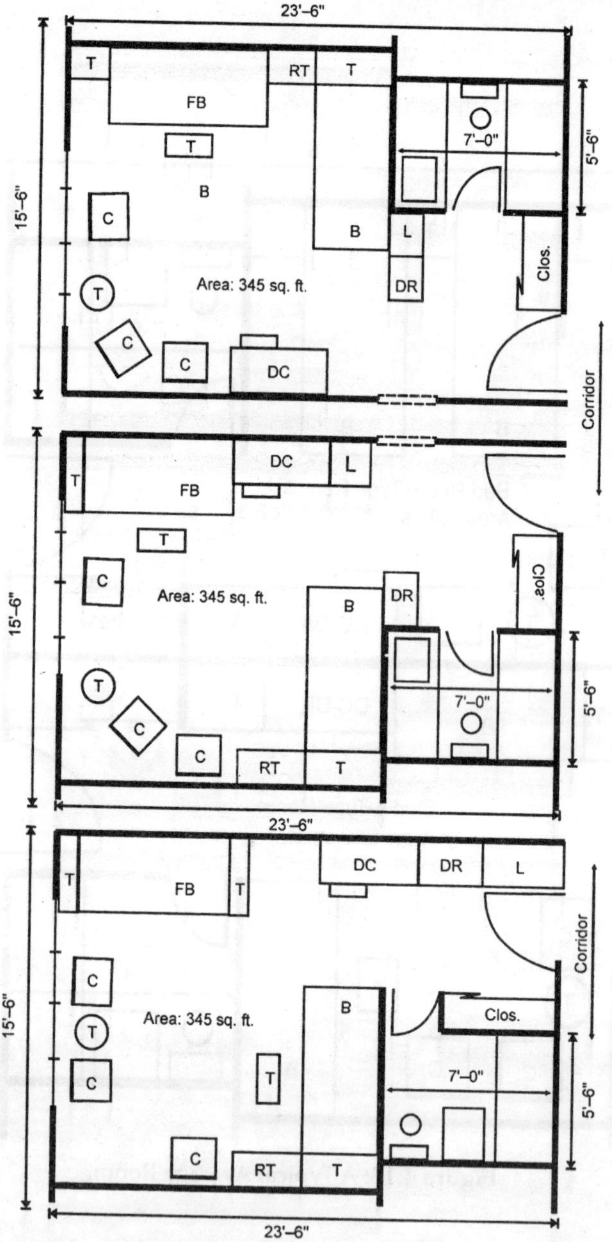

Figure 4.19: A Typical Luxury Room.

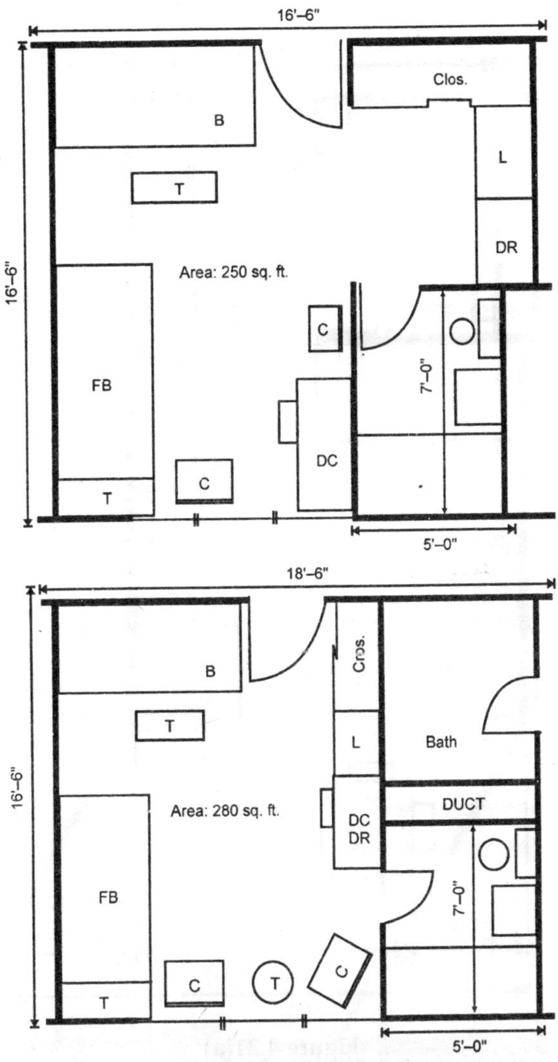

Key to Furniture		
B: Single Bed,	FB: Folding Bed,	C: Chair,
T: Table,	DC: Desk and Chair,	DR: Dresser,
L: Luggage Rack,	DTC: Dining Table and Chairs,	
RT: Radio-phonograph or Television.		

Figure 4.20: A Typical Rooms with Outside-Wall Baths.

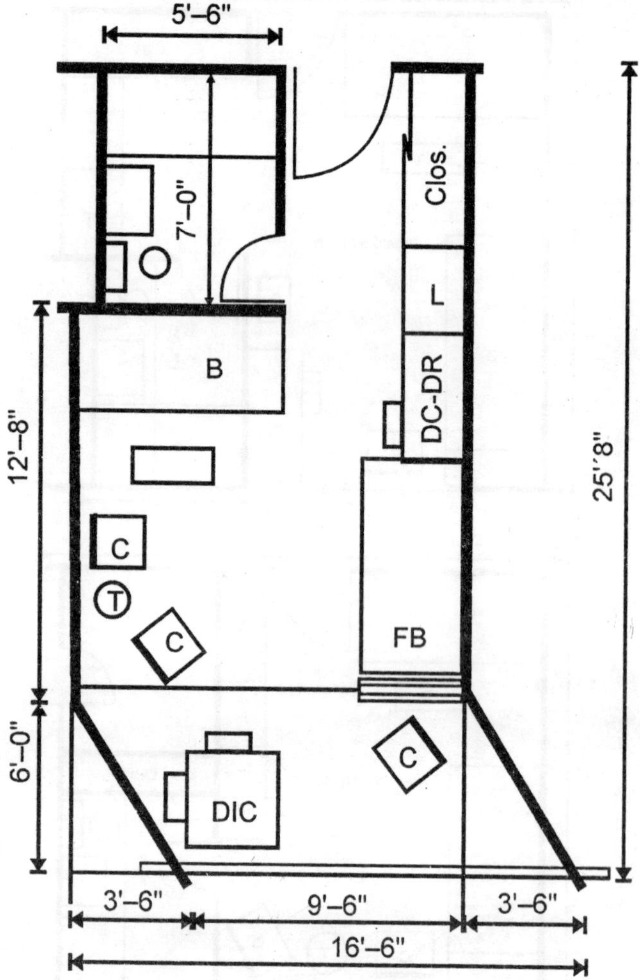

Figure 4.21(a)

Minimum room about 300 sq. ft. in floor area. Balcony wall turned for view or Dresser.

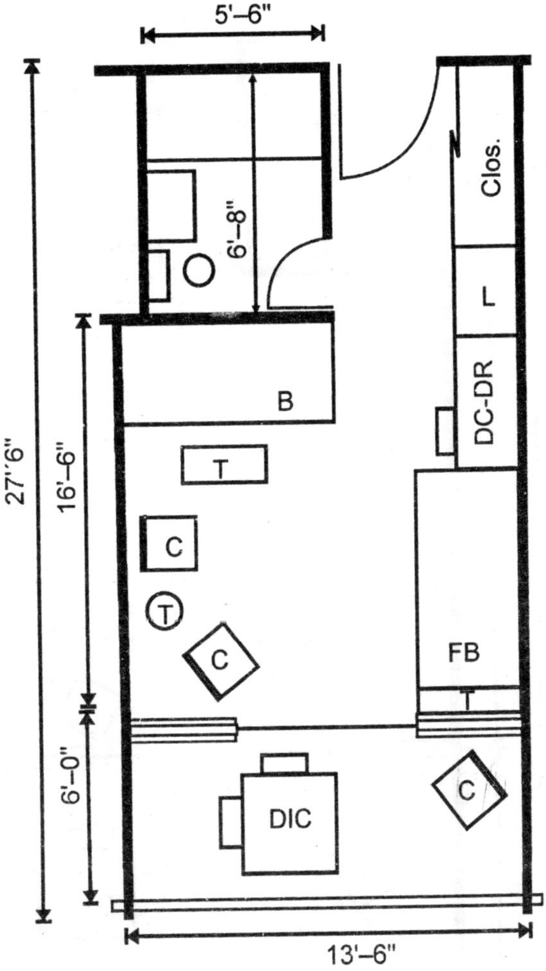

Figure 4.21(b)

All Rooms show sliding glass doors to balconies. Average room about 325 sq. ft. in floor area.

Key to Furniture		
B: Single Bed,	FB: Folding Bed,	C: Chair,
T: Table,	DC: Desk and Chair,	DTC: Dining Table and Chairs,
DR: Dresser,	L: Luggage,	RT: Radio-phonograph or Television.

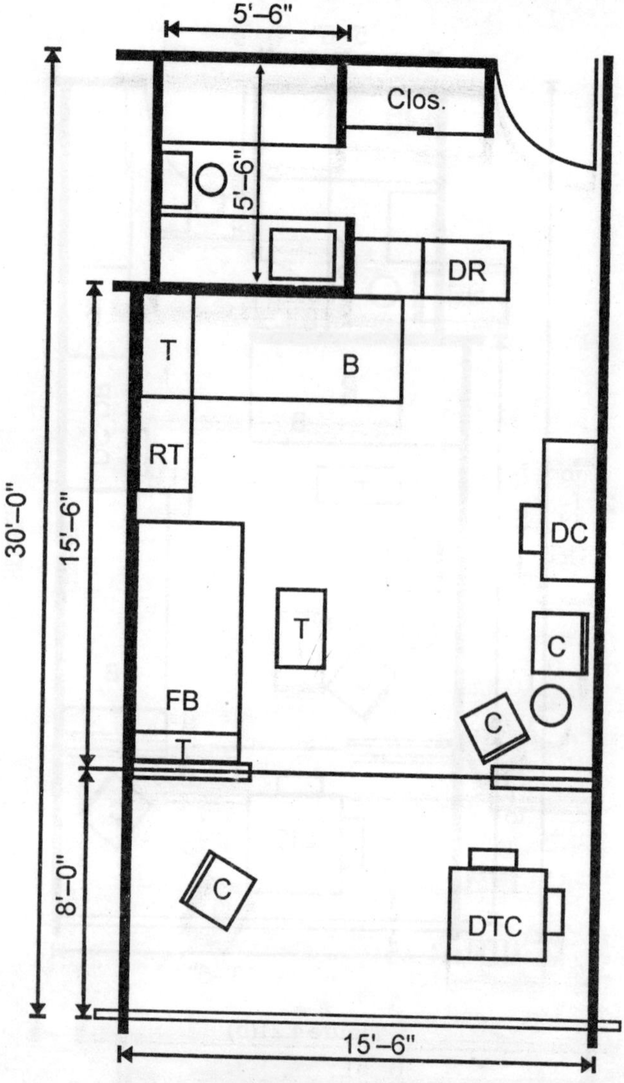

Figure 4.21(c)

Luxury room about 430 sq. ft. in floor area.

Figure 4.21(a), (b) and (c): Typical Rooms with Balconies.

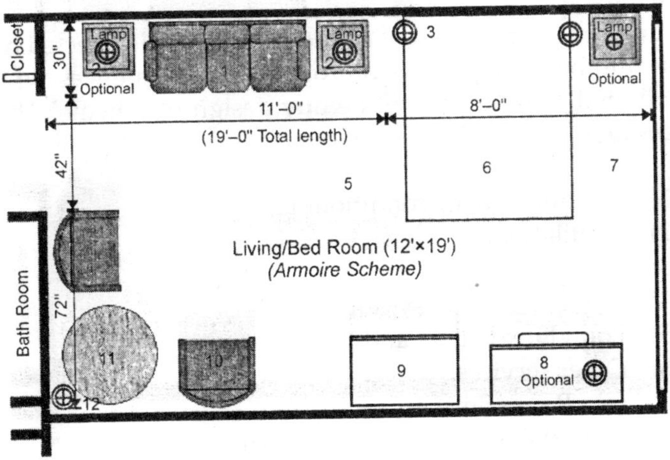

Key	
1. Sofa Bed 68"m × 34"d	2. End Table of Telephone
3. Pen up Lamps	4. Ash Tray Cube 15' × 15" × 21
5. Open Weave Drape	6. Double Bed (or Oven)
7. Open Weave & Black out Drape	8. Persons Table/Bench
9. Armoire	10. Lounge Chair
11. Party Table 36" Round	12. Floor Lamp

Figure 4.22: A Typical Floor Plans for a Living/Bedroom [12″ × 19″].

Figure 4.23: The Master Bedroom of the "Suite" Complete with Bath.

Provision of Guest Room Services

The internal environment of a hotel guest room is affected by a large number of factors. Comfort and conveniences which contributed significantly to the any design of scheme. These factors are:

1) Heating and air-conditioning,
2) Ventilation,
3) Lighting,
4) Communication system,
5) Sound insulation, and
6) Other services.
   (*i*) Room finishes
      (*a*) Colour, pattern and texture
      (*b*) Exterior and interior planning
      (*c*) Structured finishes
      (*d*) Ceilings
      (*e*) Walls
      (*f*) Floors
   (*ii*) Furnishings and Fabrics
      — Carpeting- Fabrics
   (*iii*) Furniture
   (*iv*) Miscellaneous accessories.

Heating

In most hotels, the normal method of air treatment involves heat transfer through low-pressure hot water filled radiators strategically placed throughout the hotel. This method utilises a central heat source, fired either by oil, gas, electricity or solid fuel. Radiators are normally placid under windows or against other areas where fresh air can enter the building. This encourages a natural flow of fresh warmed air within rooms and other spaces in the building. Accurate control over room temperature is rarely possible with this type of installation. However, the system can be fairly responsive to sudden changes in heating requirements. This involves the use of slim-line pressed steel radiators of low water capacity linked with a forced circulation system. Individual control over heating level is thus possible, especially in bedroom areas.

Air-conditioning

Air-conditioning involves full control over temperature, humidity and the number of air changes. Acceptable interior temperatures range from 15-16°C for bedrooms, to 18-20°C for public areas in the hotel. The relative humidity at any of these temperatures should be in the range of 50-70 per cent.

Ventilation

In most hotels natural ventilation is provided through windows and other openings. In urban areas, with high air pollution and noise level problems, a system of mechanical ventilation is essential particularly for internal areas requiring frequent air changes, that is toilet, kitchen and private bathrooms. These problems can be best be solved by air-conditioning as this seals the building from its external environment and only supplies sufficient filtered and cleaned air at the required humidity and temperature for the individual need of room within the building.

Table 4.1 gives the average temperature, humidity and number of air changes recommended for difficult areas within the hotel.

Corridors

The design of corridors on bedroom floors demands special considerations. In this area, where natural lighting is generally non-existent, provision should be made of artificial illumination and interior finishes should be handled discreetly in order to create visual interest. Corridors must be wide enough to admit the room-maid's service and cleaning trolley and to permit easy circulation for guests and staff.

Service Rooms

The planning of service rooms and store rooms in bedroom areas demand that a close attention be given to the function and operation of each area. The room maid's service pantry is used for combined functions of linen, equipment. Crockery and silverware storage, preparation of beverages and light meals, flower arranging, receiving supplies from other departments, storage of cleaning trolley and washing up of dirty tableware. The interrelation of each of these functions require a careful appraisal of the design and layout of the service room.

Walls

Plaster work: A wide variety of finishes may be applied to smooth plaster finish wall surfaces.

1) *Paint*: It is available in wide range of colours and textures:
   - (*i*) Emulsion paints
   - (*ii*) Water paint—not washable
   - (*iii*) Oil bound water paint—washable
   - (*iv*) Cement paints—used in new plaster surface or concrete
   - (*v*) Multi-coloured paints—suitable for washrooms and toilets
2) *Wallpapers*: This is used to give colour, pattern and even texture to wall surfaces. Different type include:
   - (*i*) Water resistant or water repellent papers: PVC or similar synthetic material may be cleaned and wiped down frequently.
   - (*ii*) Surface printed papers: not washable.
   - (*iii*) *Wallpapers*: Flooded to give textural effect.
   - (*iv*) Metallic papers.
   - (*v*) *Fabric papers*: Made with silk or some other fabric to give textural interest.
   - (*vi*) Embossed textured paper.
3) *Wood finish* (as a veneer or panelling) gives rich textural interest. May be polished or created to yield high gloss, satin or matt finish.

4) *Natural stone or brick work.*
5) *National concrete.*
6) *Composition tiles.*
7) *Terrazzo.*

Exterior and Interior Planning

The hotel uses experts to be entertained by his surroundings. The building as a whole can be made to contribute as much to the design expression as the detail of each interior. A common theme may extend from the external appearance of the hotel right through to the design of tables are:

Structural Finishes

Some of the most common materials found in hotel interiors are:

1) Ceilings

(*a*) *Plastered and plastered board*: Papered and painted with water paint, distemper or emulsion paint.
(*b*) *Tiles*: Decorative finishes can be applied to plaster to create texture and pattern including acoustic tiles.
(*c*) *Wooden or suspended ceilings*: Suspended ceilings can be used to drop the normal ceiling height or to camouflage unattractive features. Acoustics can be modified by careful sitting of a suspended ceiling.
(*d*) *Light domes or panels*: Designed to admit natural or artificial lighting cleaning and maintenance access should be designed into the unit, as dirt and debris reduce lighting efficiency and cause an unsightly appearance to the fitting.
(*e*) *Exposed structural elements*: The basic architectural shape of the building could be used to provide interesting and imagination interior cuttings. This technique is particularly applicable to the public and banqueting areas of the hotel.

Cross walls between bedrooms should be such as to control the level of noise passing from room to room, and fixed minimum volume control on guest room radio/television can reduce disturbance to tolerable levels. Impact noise largely derives from hanging doors and machinery. Vibrations, carpeted floors and heavy drapes will help to absorb such noises, and scrubber plates filled to ventilation and extract ducts will eliminate irritating mechanical whines and the passage of sounds between adjoining bedrooms.

2) *Other Services*

Other services to be provided in all hotels development include:

(*i*) Electricity for lighting and power purposes for lifts and heavy equipment.
(*ii*) Sanitation including water supply, drainage and waste, soil and refuse disposal.
(*iii*) Gas for localised heating in guest rooms.
(*iv*) Safety and fire prevention measures.

3) *Room Finishes*

When the consumer 'buys' his overnight accommodation, he expects a comfortable bed, an undisturbed night, rest and a wide range of support features and amenities, such as bar, restaurant and personal staff services. He expects to find a certain atmosphere or ambience. Hotel interiors have to be excitingly treated and should be able to offer the guest a unique and possibly a different, experience from that of his own have environment. Hotels must reach the forefront in standards of comfort and excellence.

4) *Exterior Design*

In our daily life we are exposed to sounds, shapes and textures, colours, smells and spaces. The interior design evokes atmosphere, aesthetic beauty and function through the interplay of each of these and other design media.

5) Colour

Use of colour may create warmth and excitement or coolness and quiet warm colours such as red, orange and yellow are advancing colours and their use makes rooms appear smaller, lowering ceilings or apparently shortening the actual length of a room. Light colours reflect the light and in consequence made rooms appear bigger. A light ceiling when used with dark walls appears to increase its actual height.

6) Pattern and Texture

An excessively large patterning, when used in a confined space, can be quite overpowering, whilst small and detailed patterning used in large public lounge areas may fail to exploit its full potential. Care should be taken to ensure that within each room, patterns and textures (such as brick works, tree bark or coarse fabric) complement each other and are in keeping with the scale of the room. Floral wall papers, chintz curtains and upholstery, rose patterned carpeting and rose wood furniture when used together in the same room would produce a confusing visual experience for the user of the room.

Table 4.1: Room Area, Temperature, Relative Humidity and Air Changes per Hour

S. No.	*Room/Area of the Hotel*	*Room Temperature*		*Relative Humidity %*	*Air Changes per hour*	
		°C	*°F*		*Mechanical*	*Natural*
1)	Restaurant	19	66	30-70	8-14	2
2)	Kitchen	16	61	30-70	20-60	—
3)	Bar	17	63	30-70	10-15	2
4)	Foyer/Lobby	19	66	30-70	5-8	2
5)	Toilets	16	61	50-70	8-10	2
6)	Bedrooms	16-17	61-63	50-70	—	1-2
7)	Bathroom	21	70	—	6-8	1-2

7) Lighting

Lighting is provided by a pendent light fitment which gives general illumination to the room as a whole, while direct illumination is provided at the heads and at the writing/make up desk. Electric filament lamps are best suited to this type of installations, pearl or silica-coated filament lamps are preferable to clear lamps, as they give a more diffused form of lighting.

Fluorescent tabular lighting can be used in conjunction with incandescent of filament lighting. However, when used alone and continuously as in corridors and other circulation areas, fluorescent lighting is much cheaper to run fluorescent lighting is also suitable for use in kitchens, bathrooms, service pantries and other service areas where a good level of illumination is required for long periods.

8) Communication System

An efficient communication system in hotel operation is essential for guest comfort and convenience, and to ensure the smooth running of the hotel, to ensure maximum efficiency the system may comprise—

1) Public address and paging systems.
2) Telephone for internal and external calls.
3) Bedroom radio system. Receivers in each room can be linked to taped music and also used for internal communications within the reception office. Some hotels incorporate a 'baby-minding' service in the system. This permits guests to leave an infant unattended, whilst a member of staff listens for warming cries.
4) Television aerial points.
5) Internal telephones, internal tele-printers or close circuit television.
6) Personal call systems.

9) Sound Insulation

Every effort be made to locate guestrooms away from kitchen and other noise producing areas. additional noise insulation measures be taken. External noise is usually airborne double glazing and heavy or cavity wall construction will eliminate or reduce disturbing noise levels. Internal noise may be produced by guest and staff conversations, radios, television, tape music in bedrooms and in public areas, accounting and other machinery, room cleaning equipment and the clatter of cutlery and crockery in restaurants and pots and pans in kitchen and service areas.

10) Glass and Mirrors

Mosaic: Used for floors as well as walls to give a highly decorative original finish.

11) Floors

The structured finishes may be itemised as follows:

(*i*) Wood
(*ii*) Softwood strip boarding
(*iii*) Hardwood strip boarding
(*iv*) Wood block flooring
(*v*) Wood mosaic flooring
(*vi*) Parquet flooring
(*vii*) Natural stone
(*viii*) Hard man-made finishes
(*ix*) Semi man-made finishes.

Some of the common finishes are:

(*i*) Vinyl and PVC
(*ii*) Thermoplastic
(*iii*) Linoleum
(*iv*) Rubber

12) Furnishing Fabrics

A range of furnishing and fabrics are available:

(*i*) *Carpeting*: The main types of carpet are:

(*a*) Axminister
(*b*) Wilfon
(*c*) Sculptured woolpile

(*d*) Orientals
(*e*) Chenille Axminister
(*f*) Tufted carpetings
(*g*) Brussels or Cord

(*ii*) *Fabrics*: A wide range of textiles and fabrics are used in hotels:

(*a*) Curtain
(*b*) Cushions
(*c*) Upholstery
(*d*) Bedding and linen
(*e*) Pillows
(*f*) Bolsters
(*g*) Blankets
(*h*) Continental quilt covers, pillow
(*i*) Slip area sheets
(*j*) Bed covers
(*k*) Bath towels hand towels
(*l*) Other types of linen.

13) Furniture

In new hotel buildings, guestroom areas tend to be furnished with streamlined built-in units, designed to provide convenience for the guests and facilitate room cleaning. Old style furnishings may be used for interior design and antique furnishing may be used to contribute a rich and mellow atmosphere. Each piece of furniture should be assessed for its suitability by itself and also in relation to other items. Plastic, fabric-glass, metal and upholstered furnishing are commonly used in hotels. Wood is extensively used as it affords great versatility in graining.

Colour and texture soft woods are sometimes used in furniture manufacture but hardwoods (such as fromosia, teak, jarrah and mahogany), English oak and walnut, plywood and laminates are more widely used in furniture construction. Furniture finishes include:

(*i*) Oiled finish

(*ii*) French polish
(*iii*) Synthetic finishes

14) Miscellaneous Accessories

Paintings, sculptures, carvings, artwork and plants etc., play their part in the design. Accessories should be designed to contribute towards the design scheme.

15) Designing a Hotel Room

Hotel guestrooms must be more appealing, more comfortable, and more convenient while designing ideal hotel room in a new hotel or restructuring an old hotel room, you remember a set of all time equipment and supplies.

It is worth having a check list given in Table 4.2.

Table 4.2: Check List: Guest Room Designing

Guest Rooms

1) The guestroom minimum dimensions should be 13 × 18 ft., outside bath and closet areal preferably up to 14 × 21 ft. exclusive of balcony.
2) The beds—two double or are king-size—extra length-with free vibrator.
3) Sleeper—sofa, separate sitting area, sofa set crosswire, can be backed up by low chest of drawers room decider.
4) Three occasional chairs.
5) Two straight chairs.
6) Party height table (27")—okay for food with occasional chairs, okay for cards with occasional chairs or straight chairs, okay for typing with straight chairs.
7) Colour TV (with instructions on how to operate) on a turnable.
8) Three baggage racks.
9) Writing disk—local hotel laws—notice regarding safe deposit.
10) Drawer space.

(*Contd.*)

11) Full length mirror.
12) Three-waste baskets.
13) Absolute blackout drapes.
14) Six astrays.
15) Balcony—minimum of 6 × 13 ft., garden type furniture table eating height, two straight chairs two lounges.
16) Door with automatic lock, dead bolt, and chain lock and 'Do Not Disturb' and 'Make-Up Room' signs.
17) Electric blankets.
18) Ice bucket and glasses on tray.
19) Phone at bed. Phone at the dresser desk. Phone in the bath.
20) Bed side control panel message light, wake-up buzzer, electric buttons to open and close drapes, clock, radio, buttons to turn off lights and TV.
21) Lighting—theatrical type, bright enough to apply make-up over full length mirror—each bed over table/ doorway/closet/desk/beds.
22) Individuals reading lights—at beds and desk.
23) Fire place.
24) Easy to find electric outlets—high at the desk—at bed—at table.
25) Sewing kit.
26) Chocolate mint on pillow at turndown.
27) Extra blankets in dress drawers—two
28) Memo pads and pencil pens.
29) Telephone directory at the phone.
30) Stationery/post cards.
31) Foreign: custom/tipping information, local currency guide.
32) Sightseeing information.
33) Informative literature—all the hotel services, where located—the hours—how to obtain activities/ schedules—area attractions—area stores—map.
34) Kitchenette-bar-refrigerator-icemaker-two burners-sink-drinking glasses—coffee maker—cup and saucers (six)-spoons-bottle opener—can opener. Utensils, plates, knives, forks, etc., available on request.

Dressing Area

1) Theatrical-style make-up lights—three-way—warm lights—incandescent.
2) Counter-top mirror over wash basin—three way mirror, hinged.
3) Electric outlets above counter-two.
4) Valet sand.
5) Wall hook.
6) Waste baskets.
7) Iron.
8) Ironing board.

Bath

1) Tub (6 ft. long) and shower with towel rack, nearly high.
2) Retractable clothes line.
3) Speakman—type shower heads, one high—one low.
4) Metal hose shower.
5) Skid—proof bottom of tub.
6) Glass enclosure or splash guard or double curtains.
7) Toilet—bidet—towel rack nearby
8) Double toilet-paper rack.
9) Wash basins (two) large counter top area preferably one in toilet enclosure and one outside.
10) *No trick knobs*—plain handles, not round, not pull-in, push-out.
11) Carpet (removable and washables).
12) Telephone.
13) Heater.
14) Exhaust fan.
15) Four hooks—two on door—one over toilet-bidet—one over two.
16) Extendable—magnifying mirror.

17) Stool.
18) Two bath towels per person—minimum 49".
19) Two face towels per person.
20) One wash cloth per person.

21) Two terrycloth bath robes.
22) Bath mat.
23) "Extra" rack.
24) Soap-large.
25) Drinking glasses.

26) Linen hamper.
27) Facial tissues.
28) Medicine chest.
29) Bath-oil beads.
30) Bottle opener.

31) Sanitary bags—four.
32) Plastic utility bags—two.
33) Disposable shaver cap—two.
34) Paper slippers, two pair.
35) Scales.
36) Electric shoe polisher.
37) Waste basket.
38) Detergent.
39) In resorts—plastic rain hoods.

Closet

1) Minimum dimensions, 6 × 30 ft.
2) Hook—six.
3) Wooden or plastic cloth hangers, ten men's and ten women's with skirt hangers.
4) Raised hanging rod, half of it for women's long items.
5) Shoe shelf.

6) Hat shelf.

7) Shoe rag—two.
8) Bug spray.
9) Laundry bag and lists.
10) Extra pillows—two.

11) Bed board.
12) Light.
13) Anti-mildew cakes.
14) Storage shelf for reserve supplies of all disposable items.

Chapter 5

Highways or Resort Properties

These hotels require a relatively high percentage of twin and larger rooms and connecting rooms that can be made into suites to accommodate family groups.

Resort Hotels

A resorted hotel is a hotel located in a vacation area and catering to long staying guests. It may often may have less than 50 rooms, but will almost invariably include special recreational facilities. Resort hotels may frequently but not always be classed as a luxury type because of size of guest rooms and extent of facilities such as dining, bar, recreation etc. provided.

Figure 5.1 shows functional relationships of elements found in most resort hotels and is not a plan solution. The diagram is a hotel of three or less floors.

Figures 5.2 and 5.3 are typical resort hotel guest rooms and apartment type respectively.

For additional room-types which may be used in resort hotels, see Figure 5.2 on "Typical Room Layouts" for Transient Hotels.

City Hotels

These hotels require a higher number of singles although the trend overall is to larger rooms and larger beds. Two double beds in a room is becoming almost standard and even singles are likely to be furnished with a double bed since it is becoming increasingly common for an individual occupying a room to request a double bed. The studio-type designed rooms, serving

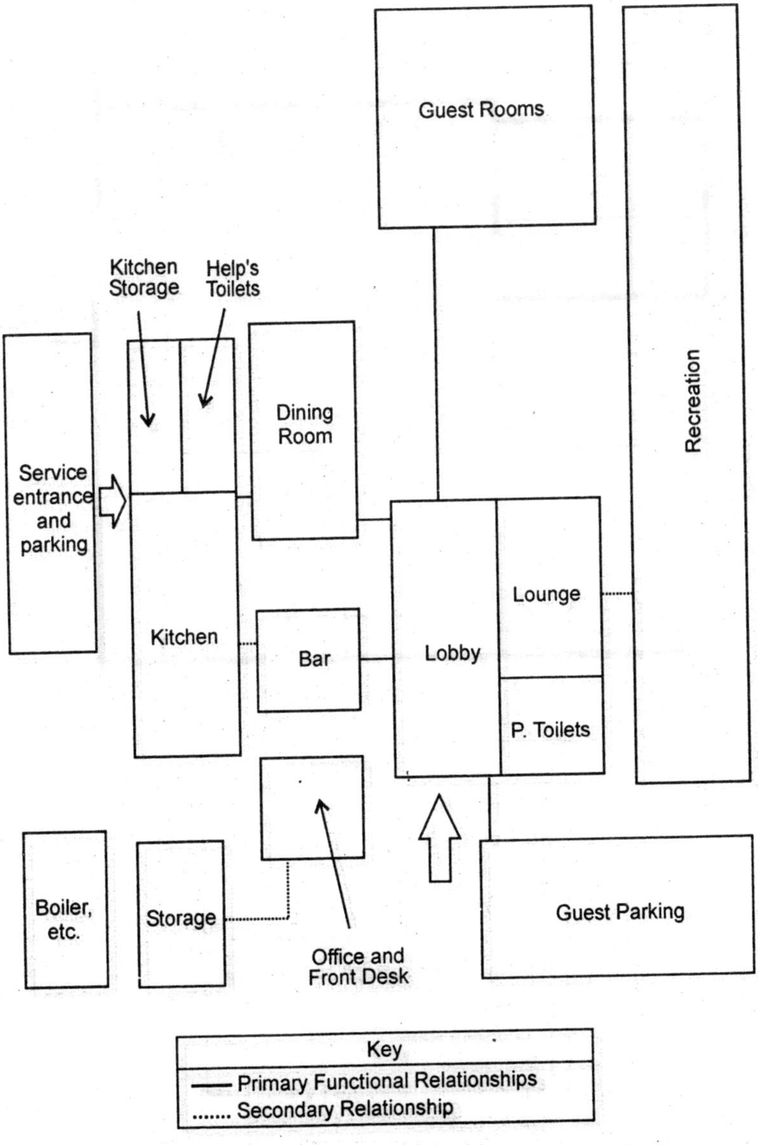

Figure 5.1: Furniture Relationship.

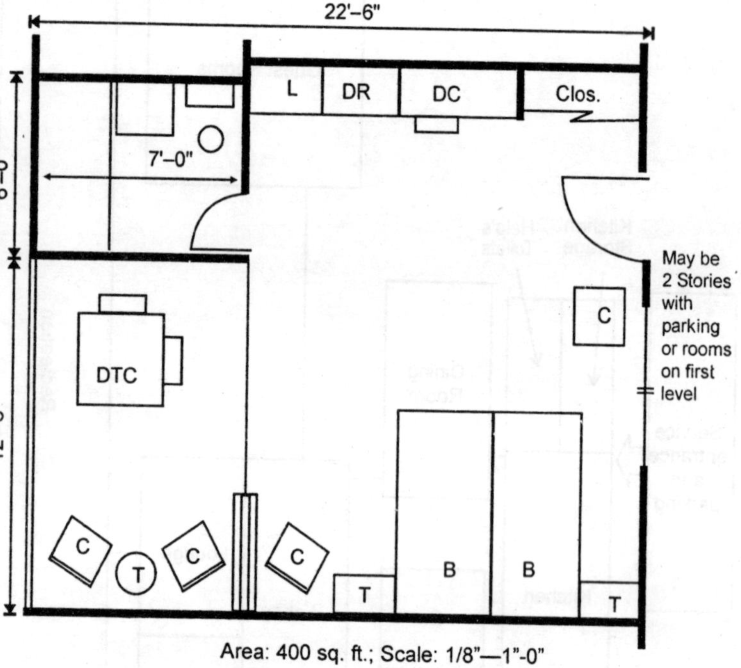

Key to Furniture
B: Singe Bed
FB: Folding Bed
C: Chair
DC: Desk and Chair
DTC: Dining Table and Chairs
RT: Radio-phonograph or Television
T: Table
L: Luggage Rack
DR: Dresser

Figure 5.2: A Typical Room—Type (Resort Hotel).

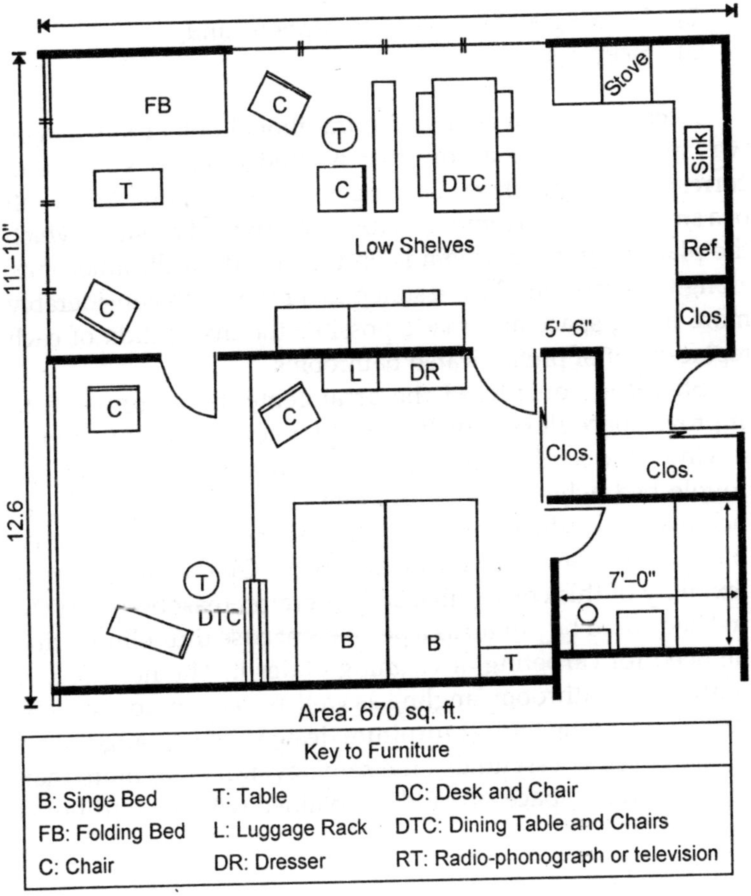

Key to Furniture		
B: Singe Bed	T: Table	DC: Desk and Chair
FB: Folding Bed	L: Luggage Rack	DTC: Dining Table and Chairs
C: Chair	DR: Dresser	RT: Radio-phonograph or television

Figure 5.3: Typical—Type (Resort Hotel).

as bedrooms at night and living rooms or temporary offices by day are not liked by businessmen.

We may analyse space utilisation from the guest point of view. Most luxurious hotels found that as regards the in-room activities the guest wanted a suite rather than just a bedroom due to the following requirements:

1) Entertainment,

2) Working and relaxing atmosphere, and
3) Sleeping.

According to an analysis, in traditional hotel rooms, there was an inordinate amount of wasted circular space and correspondingly awkward management of furniture. As a result of a study, Sheraton came up with a copyrighted room, in which the placement of bathroom is on the outside wall rather than along the corridors. This resulted in a room with considerably more living space and made possible the installation of each replacement of prefabricated bathrooms.

Sheraton considered the arrangements of furniture to improve space flexibility. It selected a new piece of furniture serving as a combination of chest of drawers, sofa and full double bed achieved by mounting conventional bed on an inclined track which can be looked into as a sofa or extended to serve as a second bed in the room. Given the potential flexibility of this convertible bed, Sheraton reasoned, that the first bed could be put up as a permanent base thus eliminating the need for carpeting or cleaning under it. The net effect of locating the bathroom, angling as well as to open up the view, and taking a new look at furniture designs and arrangements was to provide, essentially, the same overall area, more than twice the living space as could be obtained with the traditional layout.

Chapter 6

Hotels: Functional Relationship

Hotels provide various elements and facilities. A small hotel may continue bar and cocktail lounge. It may also contain banquet and private dining rooms. It may entirely omit such elements as the ballroom, beauty shop etc. A large hotel may have a supper club, a separate kitchen and bar for banquet rooms, several ballrooms etc. Additional public toilets may be near the bar and the ballroom areas. Areas for the various elements will depend on the anticipated number of hotel guests plus the amount of patronage expected from the community at large. Areas for banquet and ballrooms vary widely, depending on local conditions and hotel size and policy. A convention hotel, for example, will require a very large banquet area. In large hotel, the approximation may be made that banquet seating capacity should equal the number of guest rooms, and that the volume of all public spaces should not be more than the half of the volume of all guest rooms.

A transit hotel located in a vacation area may include travel offices, terraces, patios, a swimming pool, lockers, cabanas, etc.

In some hotels, the house-keeping and accompanying elements may be in the basement.

Figure 6.1 shows elements and facilities of a transit hotel, which caters primarily to short-staying guest, commercial travellers, conventions or sightseeing guests. Rule of thumb data is presented for:

1) Programming and schematic drawings.

Facilities in a Hotel

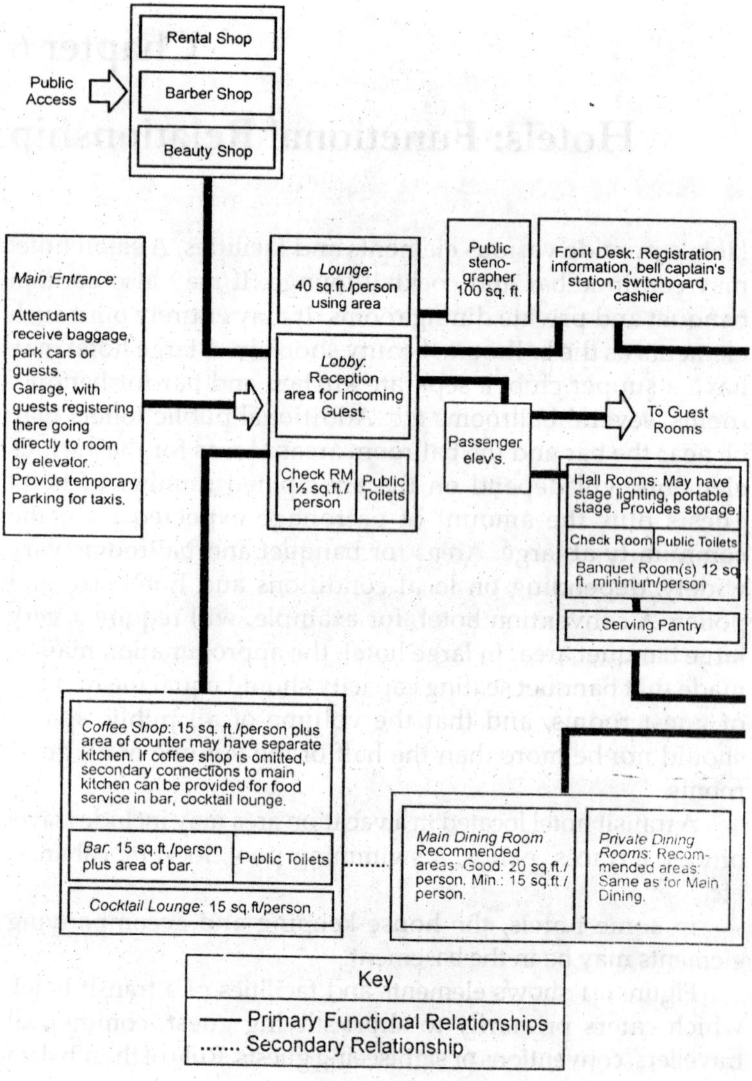

Figure 6.1: Elements and Facilities in a Hotel.

2) Preliminary sketches.
3) Preliminary cost and cubing estimates.

The element shows are likely to be found in hotels of approximately, 500 rooms, but there may be variation in hotels of any size and space requirements.

In hotels central linen room functions as a Linen Depot. A hotel usually has 3½ sets of linen per guest room; one in use, one in reserve (in front-linen room), one in laundry and one-half set for emergency use. Linen required for a guest room is:

1) 4 blankets.
2) 3½ sheets per bed.
3) 3½ pillow cases per bed.
4) 1 mattresses pad per bed plus slightly over supply.
5) 1 set of pillow plus 25 per cent over supply.

Dining room linen is stored in central linen room. This includes napkins, table clothes, table tops, celery napkins and waiter's side clothes.

Areas required in the maintenance, paint and furniture shops vary from 400 to 5000 sq. ft. each.

Large hotels should provide a separate freight elevator for movement of exhibit material, bulk food etc.

Arrangements of Main Elements

The main elements of a transient hotel are frequently divided among two or more floors. Either Floor 'A', the entrance floor, or Floor 'B', the dining floor, may be on the lower land. One connection between levels should be by a major stairway, to provide easy, direct access and to relieve elevator loads. When the hotel is located in a vacation area, any swimming pools, cabanas, terraces, etc., are most likely to work from the lower level.

Actual location of individual elements may vary greatly depending on each hotel's plan requirements.

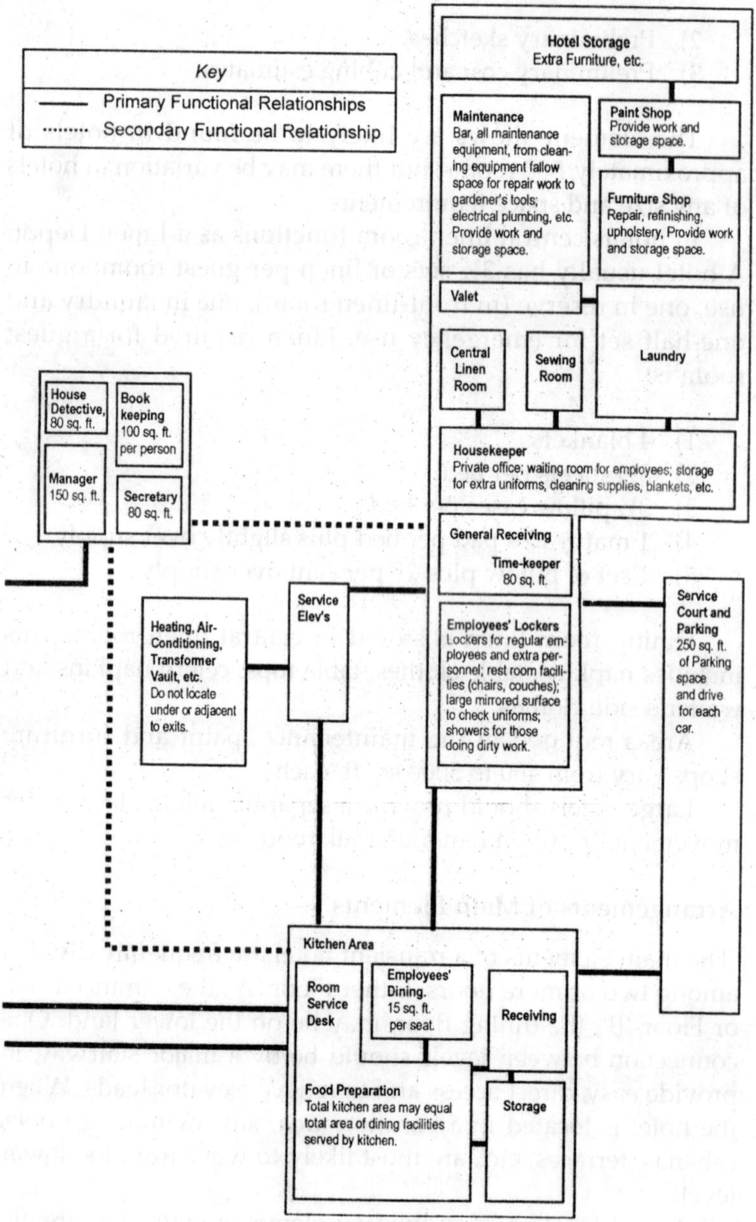

Figure 6.2: Functional Relationship.

Figure 6.3 indicate typical functional relationships among elements and are not schematic plans.

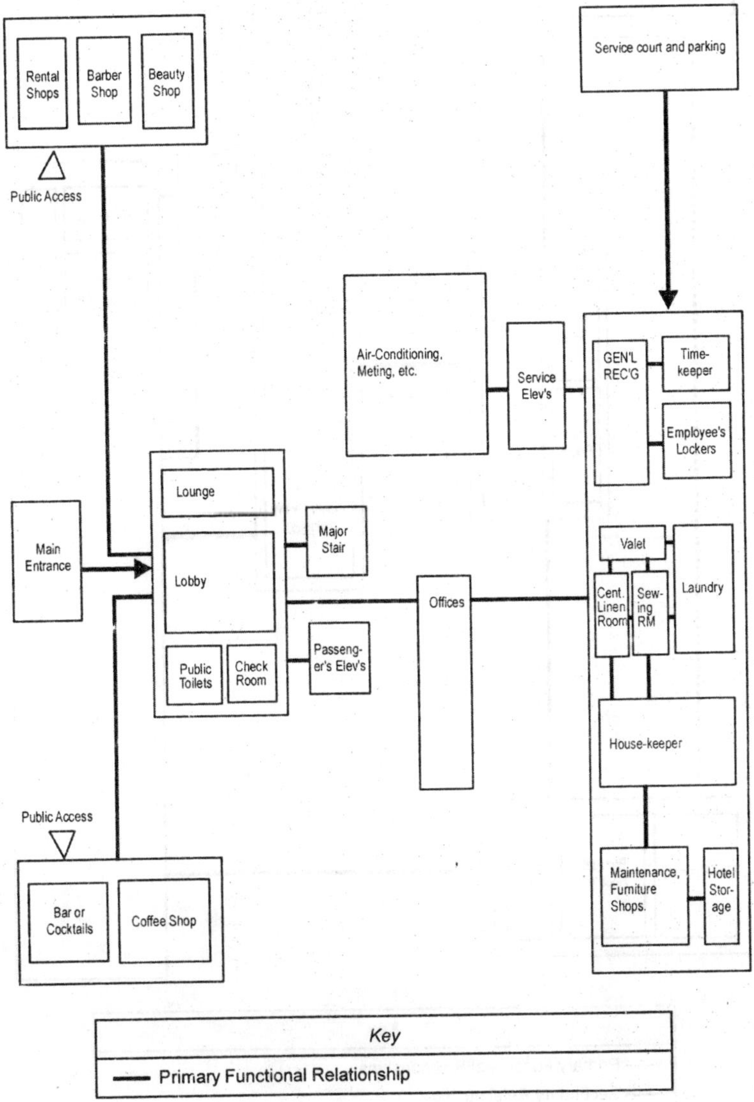

Figure 6.3: A Typical Function Relation (the Entrance Floor).

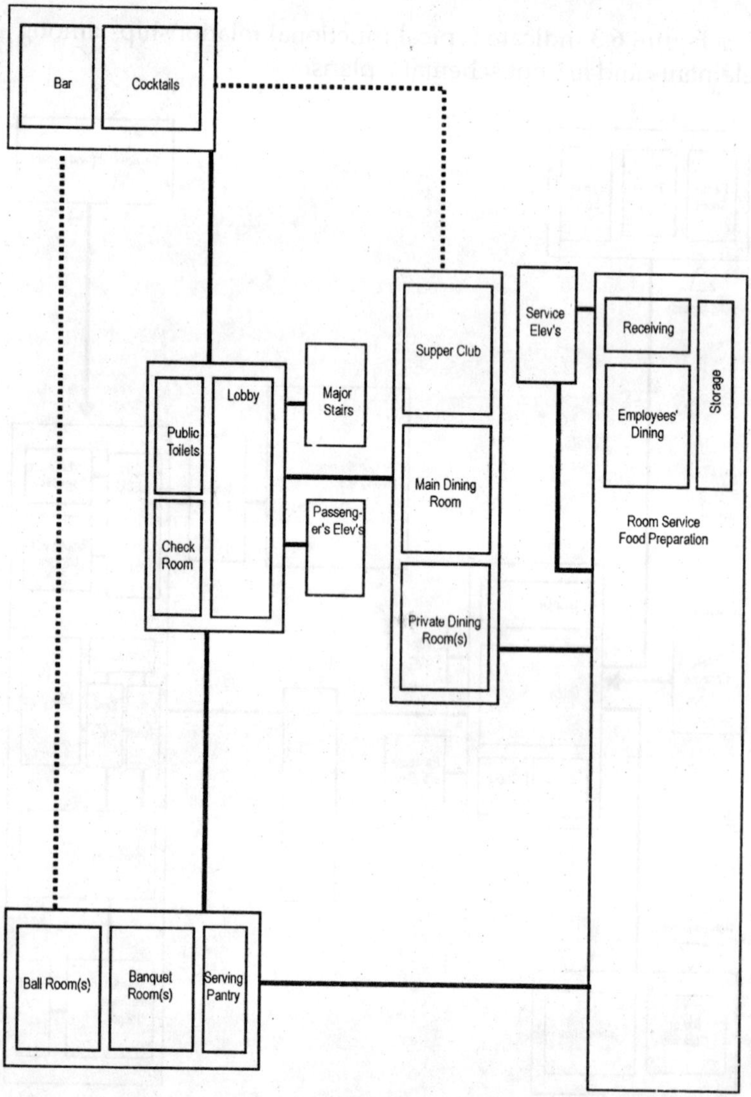

Key

—— Primary Functional Relationships

—— Secondary Relationship

Figure 6.4: A Typical Function Relationship (the Dining Floor).

Figure 6.5 shows the layout of standard equipment is used at a non-computerised front desk. Manual equipment is still in operation in many independent properties primarily because the needs of guests, management and owners are still met by these piece of equipment.

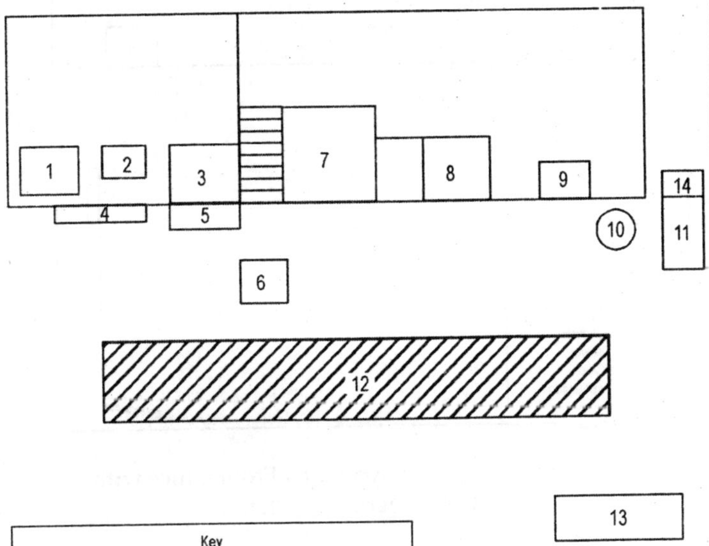

Key			
1.	Reservation Box	8.	Posting Machine
2.	Credit Card Validator	9.	Switch Board
3.	Cash Register	10.	Information Rack
4.	Key Drawer	11.	Fire Safety Display Panel
5.	Change Drawer	12.	Mail Rack
6.	Folio Bucket	13.	Call Accountings
7.	Room Rack	14.	Time Clock

Figure 6.5: Typical Layout of Front Office with Manual System.

Figure 6.6 shows the layout of a computerized front office. New properties includes computers as standard piece of equipment.

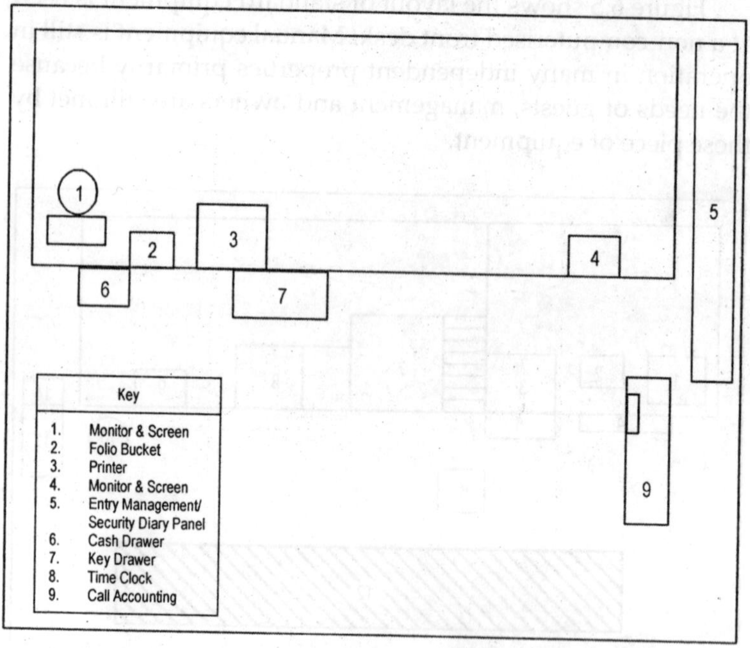

Figure 6.6: Typical Layout of a Front Office with Computerized System.

Equipment for Front Desks

The room rack contain rate and equipment cards. It shows rooms rates, single or double bed, shower or tub bath. Racks may be supplied with pockets to hold information cards. 'Exposure' is distance card protrudes from pocket to figure length of room racks with pockets add 2 to the number of packets. Multiply this by the exposure. Add depth of one pocket to this. Results total length.

Figure 6.7 is a diagram of a specimen of a room rack.

Example:

Find the length of a room rack with 34 pockets, 4″ × 6″ cards, 1½″ exposure.

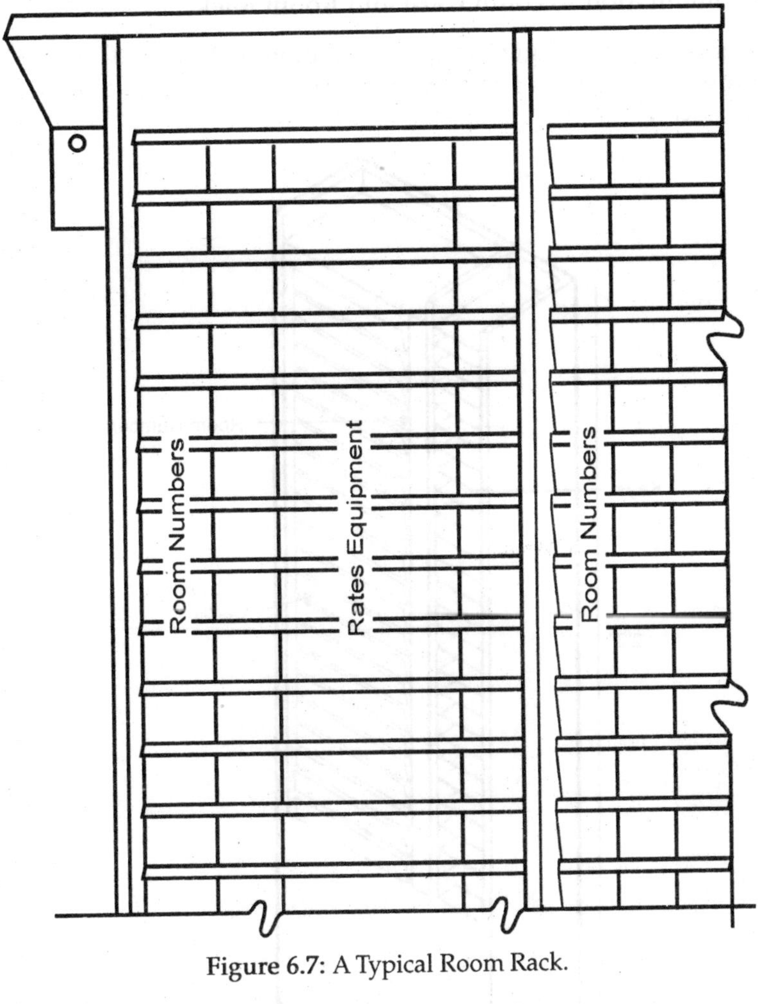

Figure 6.7: A Typical Room Rack.

Solution

To 34 pockets add 2, which = 36

$36 \times 1/2'' = 18''$

Add depth of one pocket

Total required length of room rack = 18″ + 6″ = 24.″

Combination Account Card and Room Rack

Figure 6.8 is a diagram of a combination of Account Card and Room Rack. It has a provision for 4″ × 6″ cards and 5′8″ exposure.

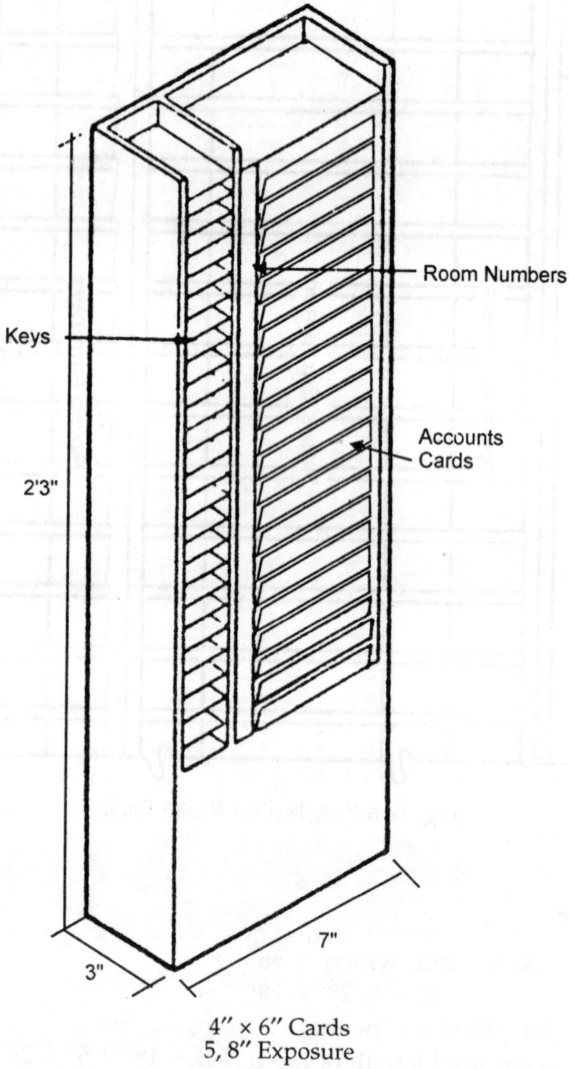

4″ × 6″ Cards
5, 8″ Exposure

Figure 6.8: A Typical Combination Account Card.

Information Rack

Figure 6.9 is a typical diagram of an Information Rack. All pockets are made for 4″ × 1½ ″ cards of name slips. Standard

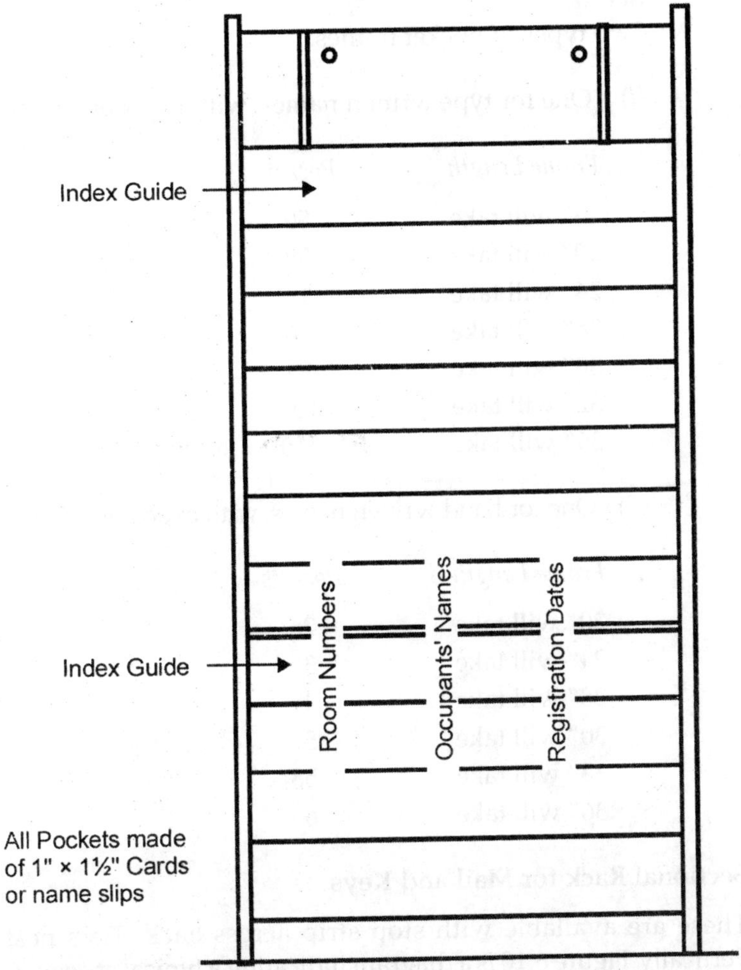

Figure 6.9: A Typical Information Rack.

rack are of 16″ high (maximum) and $4^1/_8$″ wide. Mount base 12″ from wall.

1. Closed both sides, for mounting in any position, or open one side.
2. Two types of pocket frames.

(*i*) One for type written names, with exposure 3/10″

Frame Length	*Pockets*
18″ will take	50
20″ will take	58
24″ will take	12
28″ will take	86
30″ will take	94
32″ will take	100
36″ will take	110

(*ii*) One for hand written names, with exposure 7/16″

Frame Length	*Pockets*
20″ will take	28
24″ will take	38
28″ will take	48
30″ will take	53
32″ will take	58
36″ will take	65

Sectional Rack for Mail and Keys

These are available with stop strip across back. Tiers nest vertically. Figure 6.10 is a diagram indicating a typical specimen of a rack for mail and keys.

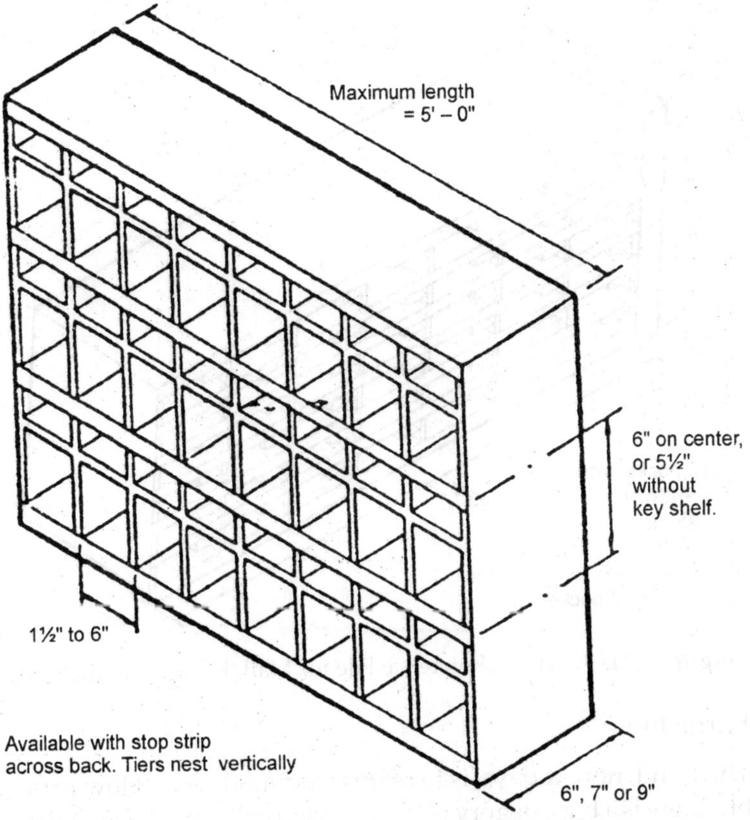

Figure 6.10: A Typical Sectional Rack for Mail and Keys.

Reference File for Mail, Keys and Vouchers

Figure 6.11 is a diagram of a typical mail, keys and vouchers for 42 rooms. It is 6 tiers high, and 7 pockets wide. It is a single pocket size with:

$1^3/_2$ high
4¾ wide
9″ deep.

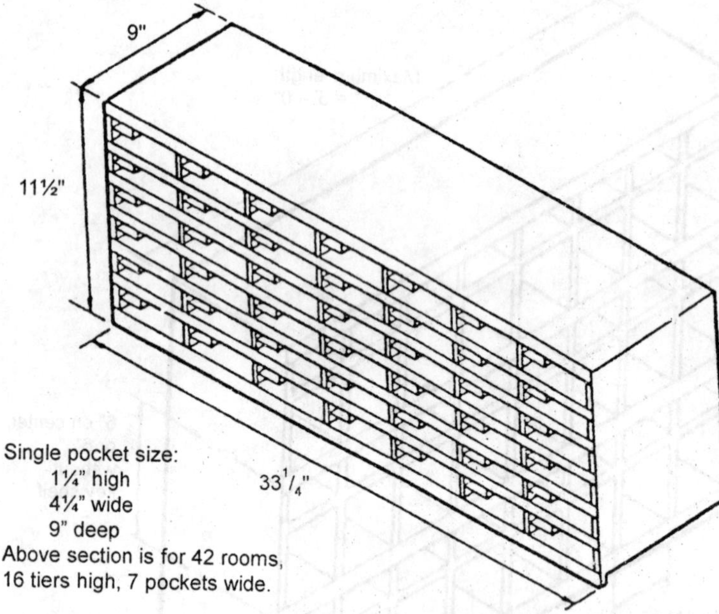

Figure 6.11: A Typical Reference File for Mail, Keys and Vouchers.

Furnishing

The trend, now-a-days, is to offer accommodation at low prices but there is a big category of visitors who still insist on amenities and are willing to pay for them. Below is a list of some items which are essential for a good hotel room:

1) Over-sized bed,
2) Coloured television,
3) Selective piped-in music,
4) Electric blankets and alarm clock,
5) Black-out draperies,
6) Game table with chairs,
7) Built-in refrigeration with ice-maker, and
8) A balcony with furniture.

Early American, and 18 to 19th centuries English styling in furniture are popular among tourists of all price ranges. Luxury establishments favoured French period furniture. The theme of integration, the furnishing of the guest rooms, the lobby, front desk, dining rooms, cocktail lounges, and meeting rooms should also blend together to create a merchandisable atmosphere. Rather than each reflecting a different period of theme they should carry out the one such as English tavern early American, French Provincial or Scandinavian contemporary.

Lighting

The main object of lighting is not just to illuminate but to create a mood, an atmosphere which makes bedrooms more restful, public rooms more warm and friendly, and food more appetising.

Exterior lighting requires illumination of the hotel sign so that it is visible at a distance and stands out from surrounding lighted areas. The entrance sign and entrance roadway of the hotel should be illuminated at a level considerably higher than street or highway lighting. The sign at a level from three to five times higher and the twice at least as bright. Ascent exterior lighting should be used to highlight landscaping and/or the facade of the building. Most hotels prefer colour corrected mercury vapour lamps mounted on aluminium poles for exterior lighting.

Lobby lighting has two main object, *firstly*, to extend an invitation to the guest, and *secondly*, to provide illumination for the work performed at the front desk. The higher level of illumination is required at the work area. It is usually best achieved by fluorescent light while the warmer, more sub-dued lighting in rest of the lobby, is got by the use of incandescent bulbs in attractive fixtures.

Poorly lighted hallways create a dismal atmosphere for guests. It may invite criminal activities.

The guest-rooms should have:

1. An overhead light controlled from the entrance.
2. Lighted closet.
3. Enough properly located wall outlets so long cords for lamps on TV are not necessary.

4) Good lights over each chair.
5) Lights conveniently placed for reading in bed and at least one light that can be turned on or off without getting out of bed.
6) The bathroom should have, in addition to an overhead light, fluorescent lamps with shields to illuminate the shaving mirror, and particularly, if it has two lavatories, an array of incandescent lights over a second make-up mirror.

Lighting the Restaurant

Basically, a food and beverage operation deals with merchandising a product to the sense of taste. Much of the success of these establishments depend upon the degree of appealing to the customers sense on sight. The light should keep food looking appetising and reflect the kind of appreciation it deserves. For example, the breakfast room or coffee shop at noon, should be well-lighted not only for a cherry atmosphere, but to stimulate turnover in the restaurant. At dinner-time, if you have sub-dued lighting it may encourage lingering but at the same time it may persuade guests to make an occasion of the meal by ordering more expensive items along with wine and other niceties of grand dining. In addition to the general area lighting of the food services operation, it is desirable to have some kind of extra light at each table. It may be provided by stops in the ceiling, cove lighting or lamps. For mood and atmosphere, lighting could focus on faces such as oil paintings, a brick wall, sculpture, grained wood etc. Proper and adequate illumination be provided in all areas of the restaurant.

Chapter 7

Kitchen Layout and Design

A kitchen plan or layout should be determined on the basis of catering policy when the establishment's over all plan is first being developed. This policy is affected by money factors—type of food to be served, the establishment location; the type of customer anticipated; seasonal pressures; possibility of expansion; greater mechanisation; development of new cooking appliances and methods; simpler operations, use of new commodities, reduced size of kitchen, development of speciality dishes on form of service.

Before kitchen planning, following questions on catering policy should be answered:

1) What types of meal will be offered ?
2) How many persons will be served ?
3) When these meals be required? Will the main meal be AM or PM—that is, will it be lunch or dinner service or day long or and/or night long ?
4) What will be extent of beverage service equipments—that is how much tea and coffee for lounge as well as restaurant will be required ?
5) Is allowance to be made for special functions ?
6) To what extent will 'convenience' foods be used ?
7) What area of floor space available ?
8) What is the position of windows, ventilation, drainage, water supply, and so on ?
9) What type of service is proposed—self-service, cafeterian or waiter/waitress service ?

Area Required

Kitchens are generally designed in a reduced size in order to provide more space and increased seating in the restaurant. Calculating in advance the kitchen area needed is difficult as the kitchen area needed per person tend to decrease, knowledge of peak, load, nature of establishment etc., need to be considered.

The dining room (including tables and passage ways) at a coffee shop may have a little as 0.93 square meters (110 sq. feet) of space per person, while a luxury hotel restaurant may have 1.6) square meters (18 sq. ft.) of space per person. Some experts believe that kitchen space per customer should be about one-half of the dining room. Small places serving less than fifty people may need about 0.84 to 0.93 sq. meters (9 or 10 sq. ft.) of kitchen space per person. Of the total area of kitchen, between 15 per cent and 25 per cent is likely to be required for storage, according to the nature of the operation and the supplies it uses. The remaining space goes to food preparation, cooking and serving.

Adequate and properly devised traffic lanes and work aisles are indispensable to achieving satisfactory work flow—one with minimum path-crossing and back-tracking. The main traffic flow should avoid work aisles, which should be at right angles to main traffic lines. Distances between key points such as receiving areas, store rooms, preparation tables, cooking areas, and the serving lines should be as short as is practicable. Aisles should be wide enough to accommodate the volume and type of traffic they will sustain. The minimum necessary widths for work aisle and traffic lanes could be as follows:

1) 750 mm. (30 m) width allows two persons to pass.
2) 600 mm (24 m) width per cart width for one person to pass one cart.
3) 1.5 mm (60 m) width for one cart to pass two persons working back to back.
4) 1.5 mm (60 m) minimum for main traffic lane.
5) 900 mm (36 m) minimum clearance between equipment and work tables.

6) 1 to 1.20 m (3.5 to 4 ft.) minimum in front of cooking equipment (to which food is conveyed by cart).

In order that proposals for the construction or improvement of catering promises may be examined before any work commences, it is essential that plans should be available for examination by the appropriate Public Health Inspector as soon as practicable. Drainage plans must be in duplicate, one on linen, accompanied by a completed drainage application form obtainable from this department. Drawings will be required showing details of general layout, ventilation and provision of sanitary drainage plans referred to above.

Any approval given by Health Department to the proposal submitted does not relieve the applicant or his representative from satisfying themselves that any requirement of the local authorities, the Building Survey Department, Fire Office, Planning Office and the public utility companies are fully met on matters coming within their respective jurisdictions.

The general requirements are intended to promote conditions that will facilitate routine cleaning, eliminate cavities and crevices where vermin (including insects, can harbour and breed, and maintain safe ventilated) temperature controlled working conditions for staff.

1) *Ceiling*:
   Ceiling to have smooth easily cleansed surfaces and to dust and vermin proof and suitably painted.
2) *Walls (Structured and Partition)*:
   The walls to be of solid impervious construction, dust and vermin proof and so finished as to present smooth easily cleansed surfaces, and where not tiled, to be suitably painted, where tiles are used they are to be properly bedded to be walls. Unnecessary woodwork, casings and panelling to be removed to avoid harbourage of dust and vermin.
3) *Floor*:
   (*i*) Kitchen. The floor to be of durable, impervious construction and to include coved skirtings. Quarry

tiles, pre-cast terrazzo tiles, terrazzo flooring or equally durable, easily cleaned materials are recommended.

(*ii*) Ancillary rooms, service areas, stores, etc. The floor to be superior posed with durable impervious material and provided with coved skirtings where applicable.

4) *Ventilation*:

Adequate and suitable ventilation is to be provide and in so doing the following aspects must be considered:

(*i*) *Canopy*: It is generally desirable for a hood or canopy to be installed over cooking equipment to facilitate the collection and disposal of cooking fumes.

(*ii*) *Efficiency*: At all times the air change and air movement across the underside of the canopy where installed, must be adequate for the size and use of the room and all cooking equipment installed. Variable speed control of the fan is essential to meet the fluctuating working conditions. Adequate provisions needs to be made for replacement of the air extracted from kitchens. Most of this should be fresh or reconditioned air and be derived from a satisfactory source.

(*iii*) *Avoidance of Nuisance*: The equipment shall be of durable construction, maintained and fitted with all necessary silencers sleeves, resilient mountings and fitters so as to prevent nuisance from noise vibration and smell. The ducting must terminate in a safe position—usually at the full height of the building clear of all windows in the vicinity.

(*iv*) *Access*: Adequate access to fans and ducting permitted regular routine maintenance and cleaning in essential.

5) *Work Space*:

In addition to efficient ventilation, adequate work space must be provided and a minimum of 400 cubic feet (discounting height in excess of 10 feet) per person is necessary in all restaurant kitchens and workrooms.

6) *Lighting:*

   The installation to be overhauled and extended as may be necessary to provide adequate artificial lighting for all cooking, cleaning and preparation purposes. Full headlights within hoods are essential. Fuse boxes, switch gear etc., within the kitchen are not advised and should be properly protected against condensation and vermin. Where necessary secondary lighting should be provided for cleaning purposes i.e., services, bar areas.

7) *Washing Facilities:*

   (*i*) Sinks to be recessed into the wall, or set clear of the walls with adequate space for cleaning, and to be mounted on tabular supports or cantilever brackets. Drainage boards are best constructed of impervious material similar to and forming part of the washing units thus avoiding dirt harbouring overlaps. If the wood of boards to be made of seasoned hard wood removable for cleaning. Tiled or equally suitable splash boards to be provided. As a minimum the following appliances are necessary where full real cooking is undertaken:

   (*a*) A double compartment sink for the purpose of food preparation and washing up.

   (*b*) A deep metal sink for the purposes of vegetable preparation and pot washing.

   (*c*) A wash hand basin situated within the kitchen shall be provided for the use of staff employed in the food preparation.

   (*ii*) *Types of Sink*: Stainless steel sinks of appropriate gauge are ideal for all purposes. White glazed earthen ware sinks are satisfactory for most food preparation purposes, particularly for cleaning green vegetables, but they are not recommended for washing pots and pans as they chip very easily. Galvanised iron sinks are acceptable for some forms of food preparation and pot washing and are preferred to the use of hardwood sinks. Vitreous enamelled metal sinks, fibre glass, or other plastic sinks are suitable for certain light uses.

(*iii*) *Water Supply*: The above appliances to be provided with an adequate and wholesome supply of hot and cold water. Water storage tanks to be protected from frost and contamination. Overlapping metal covers to be provided in all cases.

(*iv*) *Specialised Equipment*: Refuse disposal units, dishwashing machines, silver washing machines etc. may only installed where it is known that the discharges there from will not adversely affect the drainage system into which they discharge.

8) *Equipment:*

(*i*) All equipment to be so sited that the wall areas adjacent thereto and the equipment itself are readily accessible for cleaning. Gas appliances to have disconnecting unions and corks so as to permit their ready removal for cleaning. If practicable the island sitting of cooking equipment is recommended.

(*ii*) Hoods, ducting, suspended iron service pipes etc. to be adequately protected against corrosion.

(*iii*) Wherever possible work tables and benches to be moveable and not fixed to the walls. Table tops to be of impervious material free of crevices and as far as practicable, each surface in one piece.

(*iv*) Adequate shelving to be provided and shelves are supported best by iron brackets plugged into the wall surface, with an inch gap between the back of the shelves and the wall. Low shelves to be moveable to facilitate cleaning beneath them.

(*v*) Where a service lift is installed, the liftway is to be an enclosed construction of solid, sound material of adequate strength rendered internally so as to avoid harbourage for cockroaches, etc., have securable doors and be provided with access for cleaning at its base. To facilitate cleaning, the floor of the liftway to be of impervious material ranked to the floor of the room of which it forms past, the car or cage to be of all metal construction or have internal impervious surfaces and any shelves to be moveable with impervious finishes. Operating machinery is best installed at the head of the lift shaft.

(*vi*) Potato peeling machines, if installed, to be provided with sufficient sludge and peeler traps before discharging into the drainage system (where space is restricted, preparation of root vegetables on site to be avoided).

(*vii*) All machinery shall be provided with adequate guards to moving parts so as to prevent danger to the operator.

9) *Service Counter Areas:*

(*i*) Counter construction to be such as to prevent harbourage of vermin and to facilitate cleaning and to this end soft timber to be avoided as much as possible. All work surfaces including sub-counter shelves to be finished with impervious material; shelves to be moveable to facilitate cleaning.

(*ii*) Adequate work space to be provided between back and front fittings.

(*iii*) The floor area enclosed by counters to be finished with an impervious surface and coved skirtings provided.

(*iv*) Sinks provided for the washing up of crockery, glassware, etc. to be of the double compartment type, fitted against the back of the canter at unobstructed working height and provided with suitable splash-backs.

(*v*) Drainage to be provided to drip trays whenever practicable.

(*vi*) Suitable cabinets having raked or convex tops to be provided for the protection of open food on the counter.

10) *Stoppage Facilities:*

(*i*) Adequate and suitable food storage accommodation including refrigerated storage, to be provided unrefrigerated stores for open food to be adequately ventilated, vent opening being protected against the passage of flies and vermin. Sufficient racks or shelves to be provided to keep unprotected food stuffs at least eighteen inches of the ground. Impervious shelving such as terrazzo or slate is advised where fat foods are stored. Racks of metal construction assist in the maintenance of clean conditions.

(*ii*) Basement vaults so used to be watertight and have easily cleansed internal surfaces; the floors to be finished to an impervious surface vaults not adopted for any specific purpose shall be securely sealed off to prevent misuse.

(*iii*) Separate storage for hardware, linen and particularly cleaning equipment and material is advisable.

11) *Amenities:*

(*i*) Sufficient sanitary accommodating, separate for the sexes, to be provided for staff and public use. The construction of the closets and lobby approaches thereto comply with the water supply undertaking and drainage bye-laws and to the standards required by the relevant provisions of the Acts.

(*ii*) A clearly legible notice requiring users to wash their hands often using the convenience to be prominently fixed in or near the staff convenience.

(*iii*) Suitable and sufficient wash hand basin to be provided/available in a position conveniently accessible to the staff. Hot and cold water to be supplied to every basin. Adequate supplies of soap, nail brushes and clean towels to be maintained and kept solely for the personal cleanliness of the staff.

(*iv*) Facilities for the changing, storing and drying of outdoor clothing of the staff to be provided otherwise than in rooms where food is prepared or stored; any lockers provided to be preferably of metal construction and sufficiently deep to hold coat hangers.

12) *Drainage:*

(*i*) New drainage work to comply with the drainage bye-laws.

(*ii*) Where there is danger of black flooding from the sewer during heavy rain, no sanitary appliances to be connected below the line given to the lowest floor level as set by the Local Engineering Department.

(*iii*) Existing drain, soil and waste pipes to be thoroughly overhauled, cleansed and repaired or renewed where necessary. Disused pipes are to be removed or satisfactorily sealed.

(*iv*) Gullies for the drainage of wet preparation areas may only be installed in a manner approved by the Drainage Department. Vegetable boilers steam cookers etc., are best grouped within curbed areas from which drainage by means of gullies is admissible. Floor channels with gratings are not adjusted.

(*v*) Any fresh air inlet situated internally shall be extended to a suitable height above road level and filled with an efficient valve. It is to face the open air away from air intakes to the premises.

(*vi*) Any yard surface to be adequately paved with satisfactory falls to a gully properly connected with the drainage system.

13) *Refuse Storage:*

(*i*) A well ventilated and imperviously finished space, other than in an open food room to be provided for the storage, in covered bins or other acceptable containers, of four days, accumulation of refuse.

(*ii*) A recessed area adjoining a secondary means of access to the premises, thus avoiding cartage through the dining area and to facilitate collection, is advantageous.

(*iii*) Arrangements for collection should be discussed with the public cleaning/sanitation department.

14) *Public Dining Rooms:*
   (*i*) Suitable and sufficient means to maintain reasonable and adequate ventilation to be provided.
   (*ii*) Where sub-dued lighting is usual during public occupation, adequate supplementary lighting is to be provided to increase the power to at least 20 lumens per square foot during cleaning periods.
   (*iii*) If laminated plastics or any form of panelling is used for surfacing walls the material is to be properly sealed to prevent harbourage of vermin, particularly cockroaches.

15) *General:*
   (*i*) No food room to be used as sleeping place and no sleeping place to be used as a food room.
   (*ii*) Nothing in these requirements to be constructed as giving impression to use the kitchen in a basement as a 'bakehouse', as defined in the Factories Act.
   (*iii*) A permanently constructed display panel in a position readily accessible to all staff is advised to the display of statutory notices.
   (*iv*) *Liquor Licences*: If the sale of liquor is intended, application should be made to the Excise and Licensing Authority.
   (*v*) *Refreshment House Licence*: A licence is necessary and application should be made to the local authority. Adequate sanitary accommodation for the public is necessary.

Hygiene

From time-to-time regulations are made having the force of law relating to handling of food. In the regulations a difference is made between 'open food' and others. 'Open food' is food that has not an adequate artificial or natural cover. For example, a banana which has its skin removed is an open food and one which has its skin on is not.

A 'food room' is described a room in which food is handled in the course of running a business, but does not include a room which is occupied for sleeping, or a room communicating with it, whom the only food handling which takes place is for serving food in the room to the occupant.

The regulations make a general provision that no business where food is handled may be carried on in insanitary premises. Equipment used must be constructed in such a manner as to allow it to be thoroughly cleaned and kept in good condition.

Food must not be taken away frdm the business premises to be prepared in private premises for use in the business. There are exceptions, but generally these could not be applicable to the circumstances of an hotel or catering business.

In addition to general requirements, these are specific practices which must be observed. Food must not be placed where it is likely to be contaminated. If it is placed in a forecourt or yard, it must be eighteen inches from the ground unless it is adequately protected. Food which is unfit for human consumption must be kept apart form other food.

Handling

Persons who handle food must keep clean all part of their person which are likely to come into contact with food, and their clothing must be clean. Cuts or abrasions must be covered with water proof dressing. They must not spit nor must tobacco or sniff be used whilst handling open food or whilst they are in food room. Clean and washable protective clothing (overalls) must be used for persons handling open food. If the food is likely to come into contact with the head or neck, then these must be protected in a similar fashion. Waiters are not subject to these requirements.

If any articles which are likely to contaminate food are carried in the same container as food, adequate precaution must be taken to avoid contamination of food.

Live animals or poultry must not come into contact with food. Open food must not be wrapped in paper which is likely to contaminate it. No paper on which there is print may be used for wrapping food, unless the printed paper is specially treated.

Food handlers who become aware that they are suffering from any infection that is likely to cause food poisoning must notify the person running the business, and that person must inform the health offices of the district. If the person running the business is so infected he must inform the health officer of this.

Water Supply

There is a general provision in the regulation that all premises must have a sufficient clean and wholesome supply of water to enable them to carry out the requirements of the regulations. In a food room where often food is being prepared there must be an adequately supply of hot water for the washing of the food and equipment. Sink and other facilities, however, in which only fish, fruit or vegetables are handled, need only be supplied with cold water. As long as appropriate bactericidal agents are used, ice-cream formers or servers may be dealt with in cold water sinks.

Person handling food must have easy access to basins for washing their hands. If open food is dealt with, then there must be hot water available for this purpose. Soup or detergent, nail brushes and clean towels or other drying facilities must be provided. The facilities must be kept clean and in working order, and they must not be used for any other purposes.

Sanitation

Adequate sanitary conveniences, well-lighted and ventilated and kept clean and in good order must be provided, and must be so positioned that no offensive odour from them can get into a food room.

No food room must have a sanitary convenience in it, and a food room in which open food is dealt with must not open directly into a room where there is a sanitary convenience.

Near each sanitary convenience a notice must be displayed requesting the users to wash their hands after use of the convenience.

First Aid

Adequate and suitable first and material must be kept in an accessible place for the use of food handlers.

There must be accommodation for footwear and clothing which the food handlers do not use during their work, they must be kept only in this. If the accommodation is in food room, it must consist of lockers and cupboards.

A food room must not be used for sleeping accommodation, and must not open directly on to a room used for sleeping accommodation. It must also be adequately ventilated and will lit.

In a food room no refine or filth must be allowed to accumulate. This means that waste bins must not be allowed to overflow, and must be emptied as soon as full.

Temperature Controls

The regulations provides that some food must be kept at a temperature of above 145°F (63°C) or below 50°F (10°C). The food to which this applies are meat, fish, gravy or imitation cream, or dishes containing any of these, or any egg or milk. The principal exceptions to this are:

1) Bread, biscuits, cake or pastry which have egg or milk introduced before baking.
2) Food which is kept contained in an effectively closed container.
3) Butter, margarine, lard, shortening, cooking fats, a beef suet, cheese, uncooked bacon, uncooked ham, dry pista, dry pudding mixture, dry soup mixes or dry ingredients for the preparation of beverages.
4) Unskinned rabbits or hares and unplucked games or poultry food subject to these temperature controls which is brought on to premises carrying on food business, must be brought to the required temperatures without delay.

Cooked or partly cooked food must be kept at a temperature of 145°F (63°C) until it is required for serving. If the food is allowed to fall to a temperature below 145°F (63°C) and is not going to be consumed, it must be allowed to fall to a temperature of 50°F (10°C) and be kept in hygienic condition until it is required for serving. The temperature requirements do not apply during the preparation of a dish or when a food is moved from one part of the premises to another. After the preparation of moving, it must be brought to one of the required temperatures until it is served.

Flow Patterns and Functional Relationships in a Commercial Kitchen: Preliminary Planning

Space requirement of kitchen elements will very widely depending on size of dining area, type of restaurant, size and type of menu. The commercial restaurant would of course omit the room service elements.

Raw materials enter the kitchen areas usually from left, are processed through the various kitchen elements, and dispensed from the serving elements of sight. Soiled dishes, etc. return at right from dining areas clean linens enter dining an solid linens, return from dining to be sent directly to laundry or held for laundry pick-up.

Chef's office, sanitation and employees' facilities relate to the entire kitchen area.

Different cooking function should be separated unless handled by the same cook. Separate work aisles from traffic aisles. Fire extinguishes should be provided throughout the kitchen. Check local codes for use of garbage grinders and flue grease filters.

Receiving

It includes inspection and weighing. Entrance doors must be wide enough to allow passage of crates, barrels and boxes.

Dry Storage

This should not be located under drain lines. Run hot water and steam lines outside of storage, to keep low temperatures should be vermin, rodent, theft proof. Frozen food locker may be here.

Bakery

It should be separate if possible. A small kitchen may combine baking and cooking or have bake goods bought in. Store only a few days supply of flour and shortening. Shelving first shelf 12″ above floor, second shelf 36″ above first floor.

Vegetable Preparation

It is usually a separate area but not necessarily a separate room. May include salad preparation in small kitchen.

Meat Preparation

It should be a separate room. May be a part of the cooking area in a small kitchen, a meat may be received ready, cut and the area omitted. Meat refrigeration will need shelves but note hooks of meat is received ready cut.

Cooking

Equipment should be located as close as possible to point of distribution, serving counter, room service.

Cold Foods

These may include preparation of any or all the following:

1) Sandwiches
2) Salads
3) Cold meats and shell sea food
4) Short orders (specially breakfast)
5) Fountain specialities
6) Beverages.

Serving

This area has waiters pick up tables. Recommended dish and glass storage has calibrated spring which maintains top dish or glass rack at counter level. May also use under counter shelves.

Room Service

It may have a separate room, a cashier's desk required.

Serving Bar

It is an optional element. May be used in restaurants which do not have bar or cocktail lounge, or with room service in large hotels.

Dishwashing

It should be in separate room if possible, sound proof, well-ventilated and lighted. Soiled dishes may be transported on trays, carts or mechanical conveyors.

Sanitation

It includes janitor's closet with map sink, cleaning supply storage, trash room, refrigerated or screened garbage room (unless garbage grinders are used) and can washing room or area.

Chef's Office

Chief office as a separate room may be omitted in small kitchen. Chef plans, menus, order supplies, supervises cooking. Provide desk, chairs, files, shelving.

Linens

Linen should be enclosed, locked area. Provide utility basket or laundry chute.

Employees' Facilities

This include rest rooms, locker-rooms, toilets, lavatories.

Employees' Dining

This area depends on size of number of kitchen employees dining at once. In a hotel, dining area may also be required for general staff, provide tables, chairs, water cooler.

Figure 7.1 is a diagram indicating flow patterns and functional relationships of elements in a large restaurant hotel kitchen.

Flow Patterns and Functional Relationship

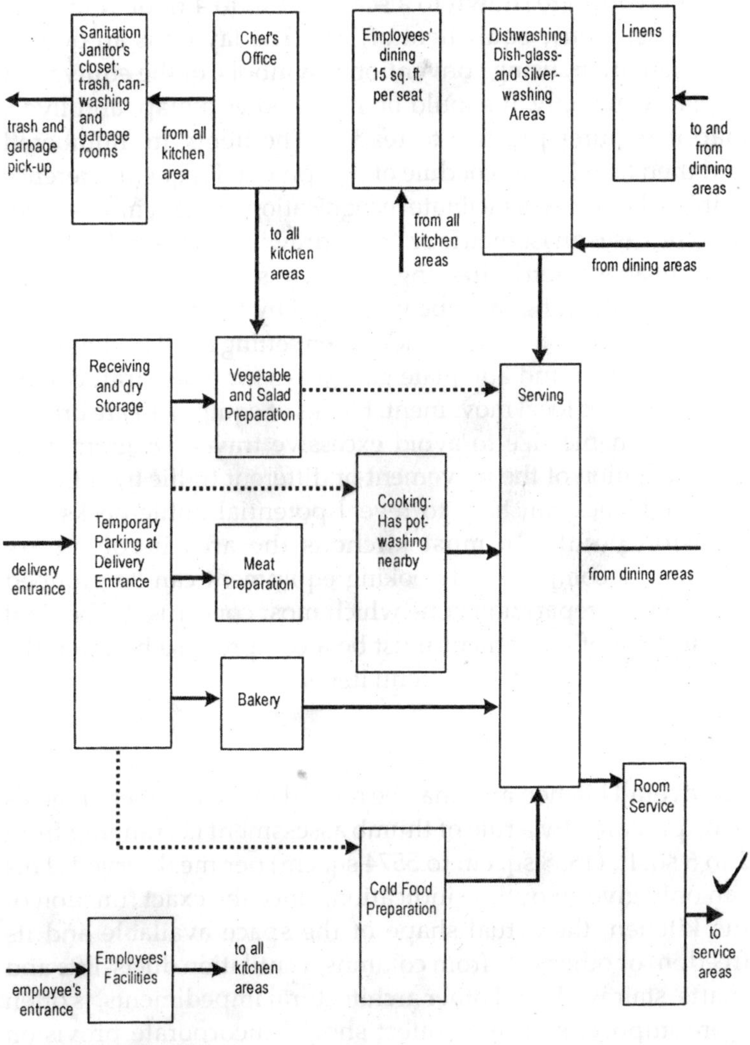

Figure 7.1: A Typical Flow Patterns and Functional Relationships.

Kitchen Layout

A kitchen layout drawing is a diagrammatic representation of the equipment suggested to meet the stated scope of function of the desired facility, within the confines of the space available. There layouts are drawn to a scale of 1 in to 4 ft. or ¼ in scale or nearest metric equivalent of 1:50. The layout is an outline representation, using conventional symbols, of the equivalent in plan view only. It should be regarded as a map, and live a map it requires practice to read it. The items are numbered and then listed on a schedule of equipment. Frequent reference to this schedule will facilitate recognisation of the symbols used. In some cases an isometric or "3-D" drawing may also be drawn without an isometric drawing, space consuming details such as oven door opening must be visualised by the reader.

Every effort should be made when setting out the equipment to ensure clear and adequate gangways for major traffic, with cross aisles for local movement. Blocks of equipment are broken into reasonable size to avoid excessive travel. Diagrammatic representation of the movement of different traffic by different coloured lines can help to reveal potential bottle-necks and collision points. In most kitchens the area involved are reasonably compact and cooking equipment can be grouped near to the preparation zone which most concerns it. The final positioning of equipment must be a compromise between the requirements of different menu items.

The Area

The overall kitchen area may be related to the number of meals to be prepared by a rule of thumb assessment i.e. ranging from 2 to 6 sq. ft. (1858 sq. cm to 5574 sq. cm) per meal served. This can only give an outline indication, since the exact function of the kitchen, the actual shape of the space available and its freedom or otherwise from columns, ventilation ducts, lifts and shafts, stair wells and other architectural impediments, is often more important. The architect should incorporate provision for the traffic and ventilation problems generated by the kitchen (Ref. Figure 7.2).

It is proposed to consider first the various sections of a hypothetical kitchen, and then to look in more detail at the particular requirements of specific type of facility. The points to be considered are:

1) Hygiene,
2) Delivery and storage of goods,
3) Vegetable and fruit storage,
4) Refrigeration,
5) Preparation areas:
   (*i*) Vegetables,
   (*ii*) Meat,
   (*iii*) Pastry section.
6) Cooking area:
   (*i*) Fuels,
   (*ii*) Cooking equipment,
   (*iii*) Boiling pans,
   (*iv*) Wet steaming ovens,
   (*v*) Ranges and boiling tables,
   (*vi*) Ovens,
   (*vii*) Grills,
   (*viii*) Fryers,
   (*ix*) Bratt Pans.
7) Kitchen machines:
   (*i*) Potato peelers,
   (*ii*) Mixers,
   (*iii*) Slicers,
   (*iv*) Potato mashers,
   (*v*) Vertical cutter mixers.

Bars, Restaurants and Kitchen: Lunch and Cafeteria: Preliminary Planning

There are some rules of thumb showing quick calculations in the preliminary planning of restaurant, luncheonette and cafeteria kitchens, although specific conditions and requirements of any jobs may change of the areas. Rule of thumb approach for preliminary planning as given in Tables 7.1, 7.2, 7.3, 7.4, 7.5 and 7.6 could only be used for drawing purposes. Any drawings to be carried out as a part of the preliminary stage be done specifically in consultation with the services of an experiences kitchen consultant.

Table 7.1: A Typical Preliminary Planning Criteria for Bar, and Restaurant—Kitchen

Dining area: Allow 12 sq. ft. per person seated.

Linen storage: Located in dry storage area.

Bar (for dining overflow): Add 15% of dining area (includes bar counter area).

Kitchen equals		50% of dining area
Broken-down as follows:		
1)	Meat preparation	4% of kitchen area
2)	Vegetable preparation	7% " " "
3)	Cooking	12% " " "
4)	Cold foods	7% " " "
5)	Bakery	10% " " "
6)	Serving pantry	14% " " "
7)	Dishwashing	10% " " "
8)	Circulation area	36% " " "
		100% of kitchen area

Kitchen Services:

The following percentages (of the kitchen area) are required in addition to those of the kitchen proper.

1)	Storage, dray	15% of kitchen area
2)	Storage, refrigerator	14% " " "
3)	Receiving	10% " " "
4)	Trash and garbage	10% " " "
5)	Help's facilities	20% " " "
6)	Chef's office	7% " " "
		76% of kitchen area

Table 7.2: A Typical Preliminary Planning for a Restaurant Kitchen having a Seating Capacity of 200 Persons

Seating 200 persons at 12 sq. ft. per person		2400 sq. ft.
Bar (for overflow)		360 sq. ft.
Kitchen: 1200 sq. ft.		
1)	Meat preparation	50 sq. ft.
2)	Vegetable preparation	80 sq. ft.
3)	Cooking	140 sq. ft.
4)	Cold foods	80 sq. ft.
5)	Bakery	120 sq. ft.
6)	Serving pantry	160 sq. ft.
7)	Dishwashing	120 sq. ft.
8)	Circulation area	450 sq. ft.
		1200 sq. ft.
1)	Storage, dry	180 sq. ft.
2)	Storage, refrigerator	160 sq. ft.
3)	Receiving	120 sq. ft.
4)	Trash and garbage	120 sq. ft.
5)	Help's facilities	240 sq. ft.
6)	Chef's office	80 sq. ft.
	900	sq. ft.
Total area for preliminary calculations		4860 sq. ft.
for convenience, use		5600 sq. ft

Table 7.3: A Typical Preliminary Planning Criteria for Luncheonette

Serving limited menu: beverages, sandwiches, short orders, etc.
Dining are:

Allow 18 sq. ft. per person seated. (Includes counter area)

Kitchen equals 50% of dining area Includes food preparation, food storage, locker and toilet facilities, dishwashing, etc.

Table 7.4: A Typical Preliminary Planning—A 100 Seating Capacity Luncheonette

Assume a seating capacity of 100 persons.

Seating 100 persons at 18 sq. ft. per person	1800 sq. ft.
Kitchen	900 sq. ft.
Total area for preliminary calculations	2700 sq. ft.

Table 7.5: A Typical Preliminary Planning for Cafeteria—Kitchen

Dining area:

Allow 18 sq. ft. per person seated (Includes serving counter area)

Kitchen equals	One-third of dining area

Broken down as follows:

1) Meat preparation	4% of kitchen area
2) Vegetable preparation	7% of kitchen area
3) Cooking	12% of kitchen area
4) Cold foods	10% of kitchen area
5) Bakery	20% of kitchen area
6) Dish washing	10% of kitchen area
7) Circulation area	37% of kitchen area
	100% of kitchen area

Kitchen services:

The following percentages (of the kitchen area) are required in addition to those of the kitchen proper.

1) Storage, dry	15% of kitchen area
2) Storage, refrigerator	15% of kitchen area
3) Receiving	10% of kitchen area
4) Trash and garbage	10% of kitchen area
5) Help's facilities	20% of kitchen area
6) General office	5% of kitchen area

Table 7.6: A Typical Preliminary Planning for a Cafeteria-Kitchen Having a Seating Capacity of 200 Persons

Seating: 200 at 18 sq. ft. per person		3600 sq. ft.
Kitchen: 1200 sq. ft.		
1)	Meat preparation	50 sq. ft.
2)	Vegetable preparation	80 sq. ft.
3)	Cooking	150 sq. ft.
4)	Cold foods	120 sq. ft.
5)	Bakery	225 sq. ft.
6)	Dish washing	120 sq. ft.
7)	Circulation area	455 sq. ft.
		1200 sq. ft.
1)	Storage, dry	180 sq. ft.
2)	Storage, refrigerator	180 sq. ft.
3)	Receiving	120 sq. ft.
4)	Trash and garbage	120 sq. ft.
5)	Help's facilities	240 sq. ft.
6)	General office	60 sq. ft.
		900 sq. ft.
Total area for preliminary calculations:		5700 sq. ft.

Installation for Fast Food Service

Fast food service is that provided by luncheonettes, soda fountains and dinettes (serving simple meals), which provide counter service and by short order sections of main kitchens. Counter service operations may have a separate kitchen with food preparation, cooking and dishwashing areas. The basic installation for counter service are:

1) Back-bar,
2) Front-counter,
3) Island, and
4) Combination of the above.

Short-Order Kitchen

A short order section in a main kitchen does the same type of cooking as behind the counter installations, but usually has heavy equipment layer than that used in counters unit at right provides a more simple service than that at left. Figure 7.2 is a diagram showing a typical installation for a short order kitchen.

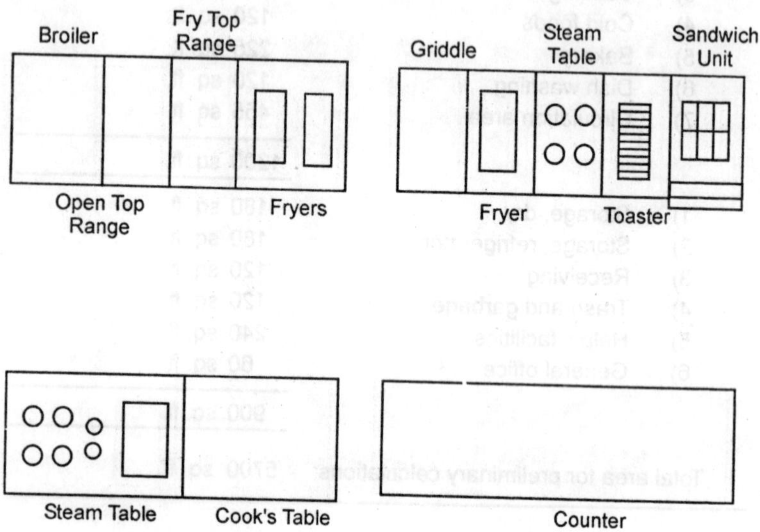

Figure 7.2: Short-Order Kitchen.

Back-Bar (Small)

It is usually for a small operation, with minimum menu and rapid customer turn-over. Has short counter, therefore, usually uses straight counter rather than bay. Figure 7.3 is a diagram indicating installation for a small back-bar. Figure 7.3 is a diagram showing typical installation for a small back bar.

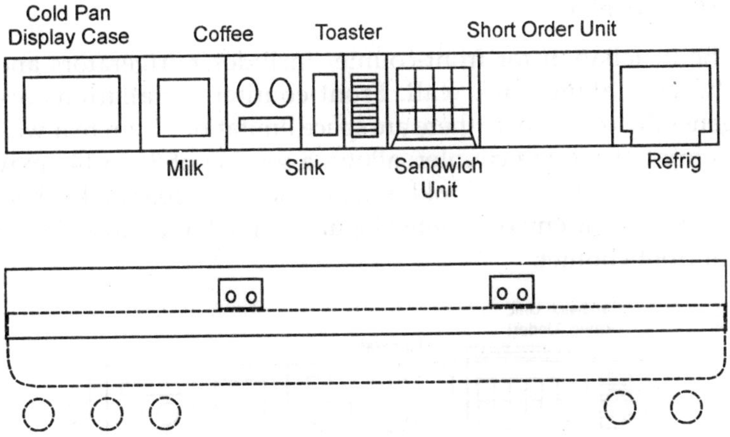

Figure 7.3: Back-Bar Installation (Small).

Back-Bar (Large)

This may have entire cooking unit in back-bar installation. Lengthy counter requires duplication of coffee making facilities. Bay counter seating may be used also. Figure 7.4 is a diagram showing typical installation for a large back-bar.

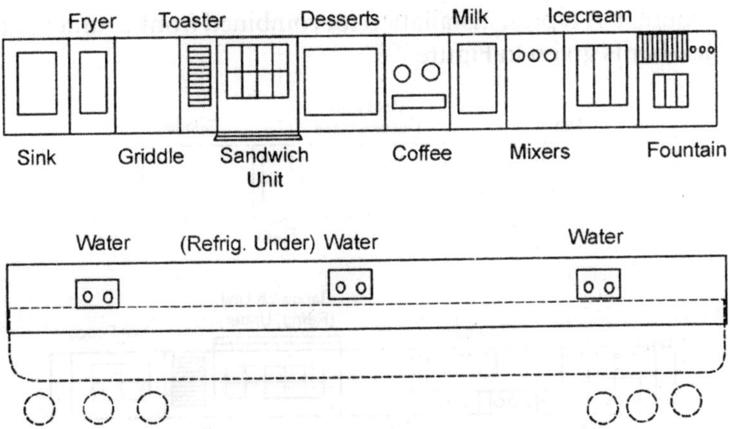

Figure 7.4: Back-Bar Installation (Large).

Front-Counter

The installation for front-counter includes refrigerators and shelving along back wall. Front-counter installations are generally used where there are space limitations from rear wall to front of serving counter; allows a serving of 8″ to 14″ may have some elaborate cooking equipment in separate kitchen, located at one end of counter. Figure 7.5 is a typical installation for front-counter.

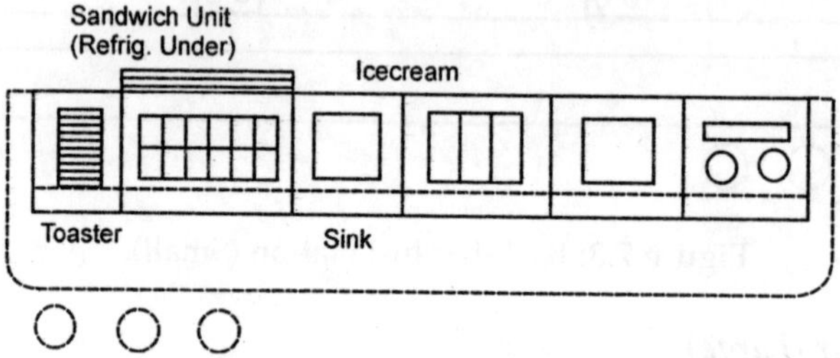

Figure 7.5: Front-Counters Installation.

Combined Front-Counter and Back-Bar

It is suitable for operations with limited area and staff, and a large menu. May serve books from waiter/waitress stand at end of counter. A typical installation for combined front-counter and back-bar is given in Figure 7.6.

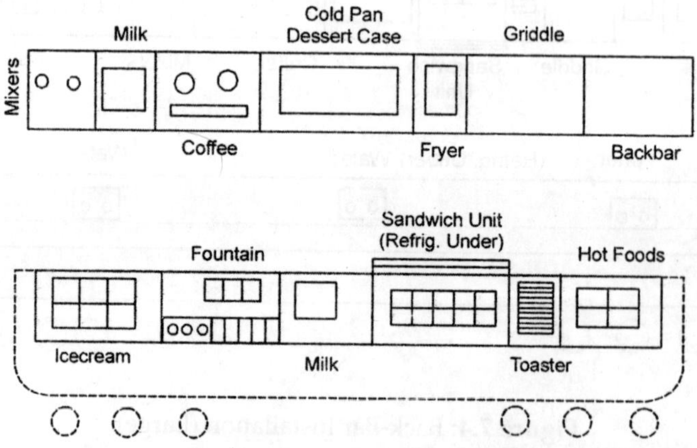

Figure 7.6: Combined Front-Counter and Back-Bar Installation.

Usually for operation with limited area and staff and a larger menu may serve booths from waiters stand at end of counters.

Island

Island installation may have straight or bay counter seating, also allows for direct booth service by counter waiters. Typical installation for island is given in Figure 7.7.

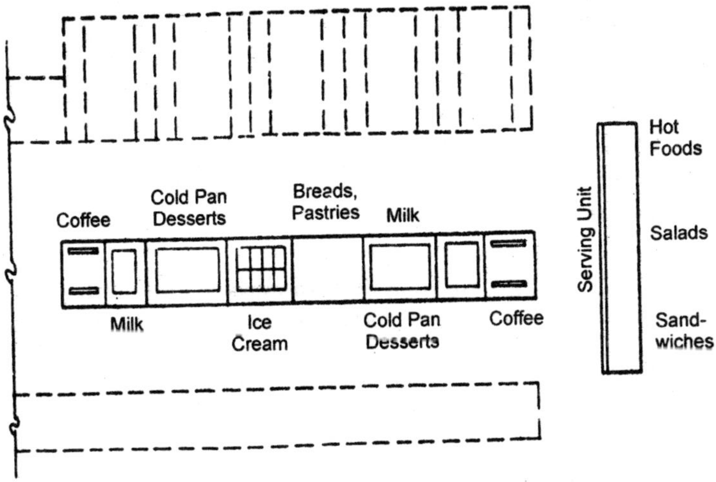

Figure 7.7: Island Installation.

Installation for Fast Food Services

Bars, Restaurants and Kitchens

Fast food service is that type provided by luncheonettes, soda fountains, and dinettes (serving simple meals), which provide counter Service, and by short-order sections of main kitchen. Counter service operations may have a separate kitchen with food preparation, cooking and dishwashing areas.

The basic installations for counter service are:

1) Back-bar,
2) Front-counter,
3) Island, and
4) Combinations of the above.

A short-order section in a main kitchen does the same type of cooking as behind-the-counter installations, but usually has heavy equipment larger than that used in counters. Unit at right provides a more simple service than that at left.

Usually for a small operation, with minimum menu and rapid customer turn-over. Has short counter; therefore usually uses straight counter rather than way.

May have entire cooking unit in back-bar installation. Lengthy counter requires duplication of coffee-making facilities. Bay counter seating may be used also.

May have refrigerators and shelving along back wall. Front counter installations are generally used where there are space limitations from rear wall to front of serving counter; allows a saving of 8″ to 14″. May have more elaborate cooking equipment in separate kitchen, located at one end of counter.

A usually for operations with limited area and staff, and a larger menu. May serve booths from waiters stand at end of counter.

May have straight or bay counter seating; also allows for direct service by counter waiters.

Kitchen Areas: Equipment Relationships

Kitchen areas have include—

1) Vegetable and salad preparation,
2) Meat and fish preparation,
3) Cooking section,
4) Pastry section,
5) Pantry Area,
6) Cold food section,
7) Service bar area,
8) Post washing area, and
9) Dish, glass, silver and tray washing.

The type, quantity and layout of equipment will vary with anticipated patronage and menu. For example, large kitchens may need more items, such as ranges and kettles, than are shown under 'cooking sections'. Small kitchens may combine in a cooking area functions shown separately below, such as cooking and baking. Figures 7.8, 7.9, 7.10 and 7.11 show schematic drawings of various kitchen areas. The drawings are intended to show efficient functional relationships of the main equipment and do not attempt to present design solutions to kitchen equipment layout.

Work Aisles

If the draft, minimum width 3′0″, with 2 parallel work tables, minimum aisle width is 3′-6″, preferably 4′-6″.

Vegetable and Salad Preparation Area

Figure 7.8 is a typical functional relationship of the main equipment for vegetable and salad preparation area.

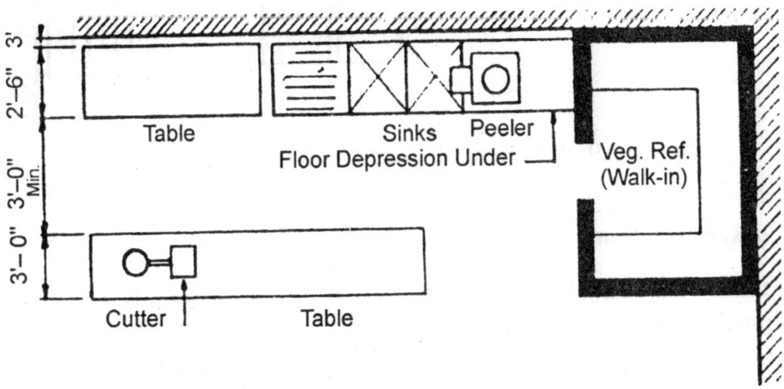

Figure 7.8: A Typical Vegetable and Salad Preparation Area.

Meat and Fish Preparation Area

Figure 7.9 is a typical functional relationship of the main equipment for meat and fish preparation area.

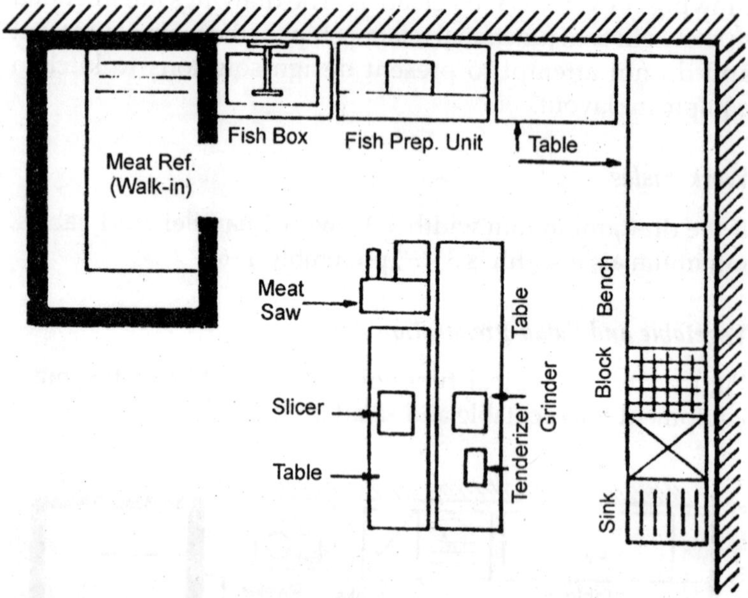

Figure 7.9: A Typical Meat and Fish Preparation Area.

Cooking Section

Kitchen may need more items, such as ranges and kettles. Small kitchen may combine in a cooking area functions such as cooking and baking various types of cooking sections area.

Island Type Section

Figure 7.10 indicates a diagram showing typical equipment relations for an Island Type Section.

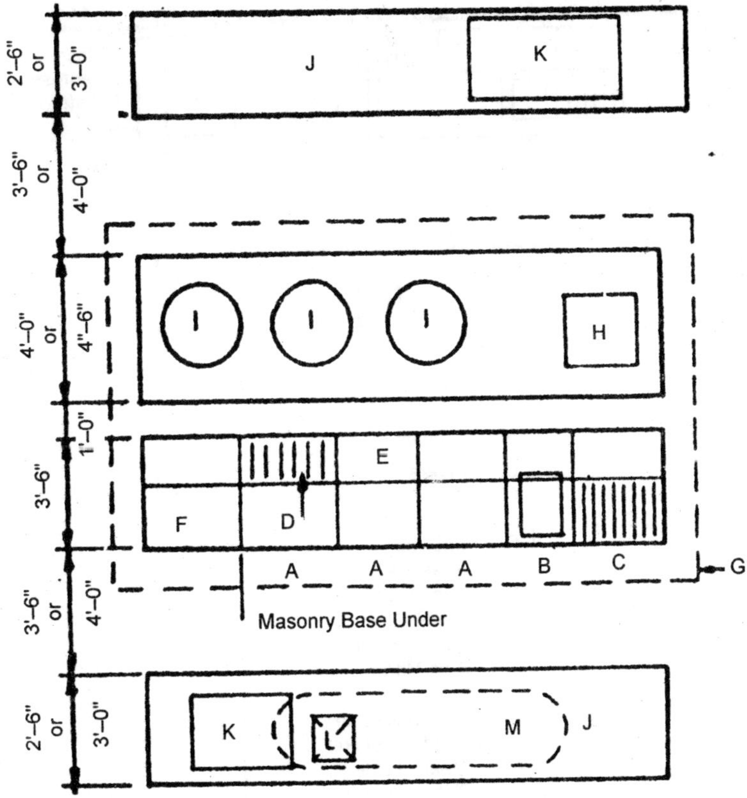

Figure 7.10: Island-Type Section.

Section Against Wall

Figure 7.11 shows a diagram indicating typical equipment relations for a section against wall.

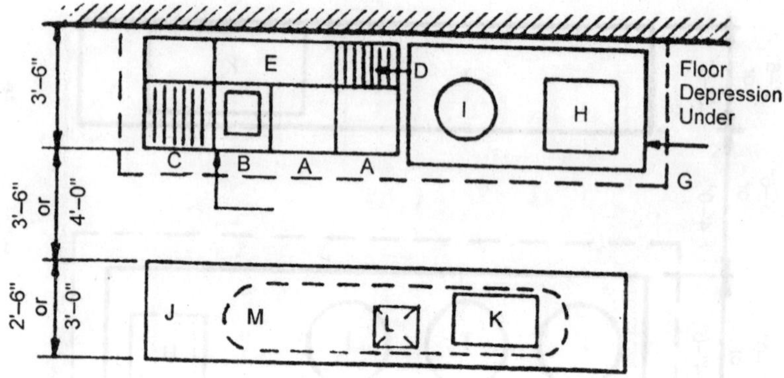

Key	
A.	Ranges
B.	Fryers
C.	Broilers
D.	Salamanders
E.	Shelves
F.	Roasters
G.	Hood (over)
H.	Kettle
I.	Cook's Table
J.	Bain Marie
K.	Sink
L.	Pot Rack (over)
M.	Short Order Ref.
N.	Steam Table
O.	Plate Warmer
P.	Mixer

Figure 7.11: Section Against Wall.

Large Dining Establishment

Figure 7.12 shows the equipment relationships of a section for large dining establishment.

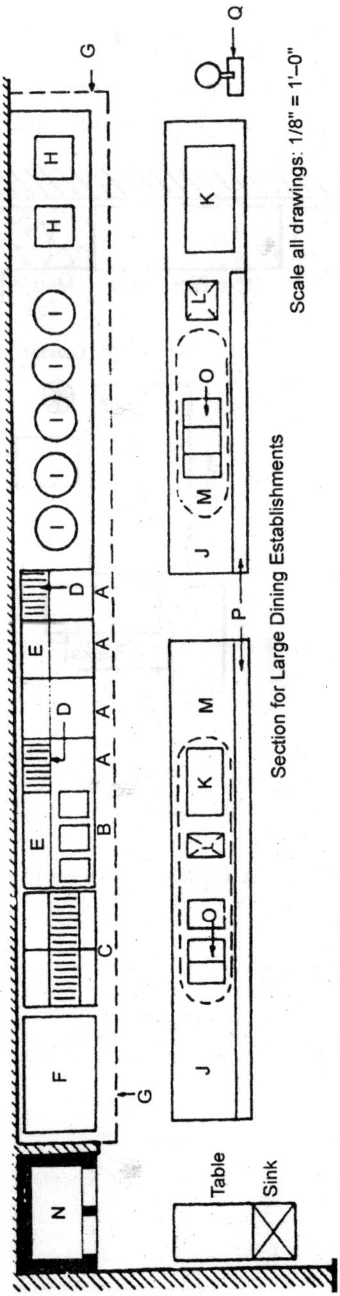

Section for Large Dining Establishments

Scale all drawings: 1/8" = 1'–0"

Figure 7.12: A Typical Large Dinning Establishment.

Pastry Section

Figure 7.13 is a typical schematic drawings of pastry section indicating functional relationship of main equipment.

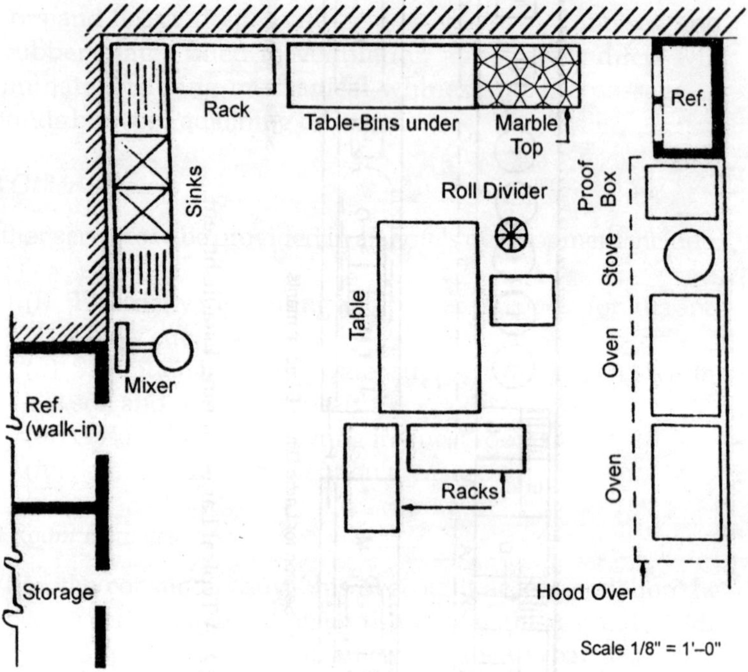

Figure 7.13: A Typical Pastry Section.

Pantry Section

Figure 7.14 is a typical schematic drawings indicating functional relationship of main equipment in a pantry.

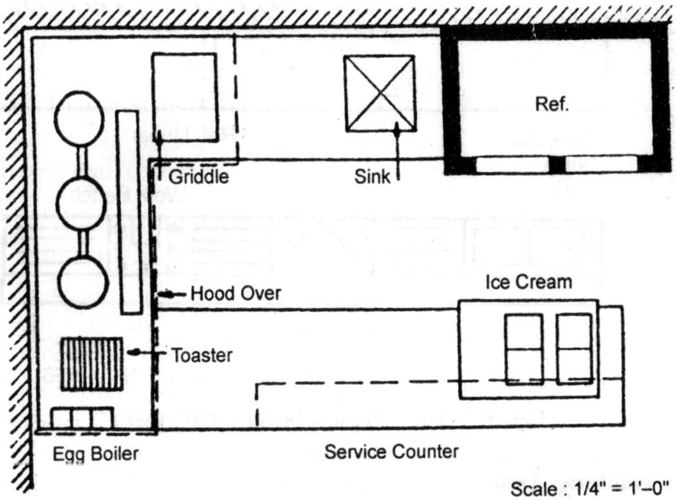

Figure 7.14: A Typical Pantry Area.

Sections Against Wall

Cold Foods

Figure 7.15 is typical schematic drawings indicating functional relationship for main equipment in the cold food section.

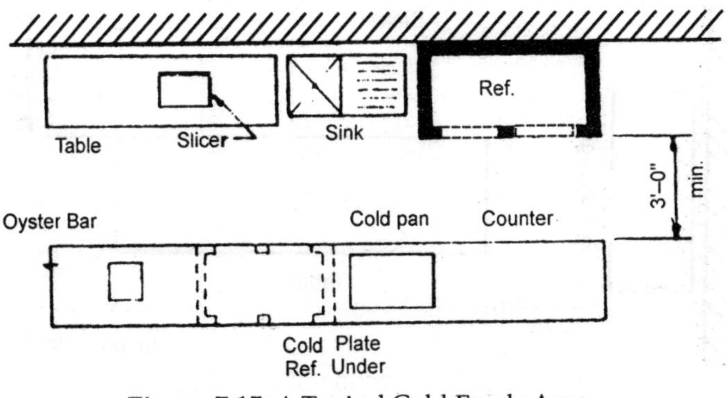

Figure 7.15: A Typical Cold Foods Area.

Service Bar Area

Figure 7.16 is a typical schematic drawings indicating functional relationship for Service Bar Area.

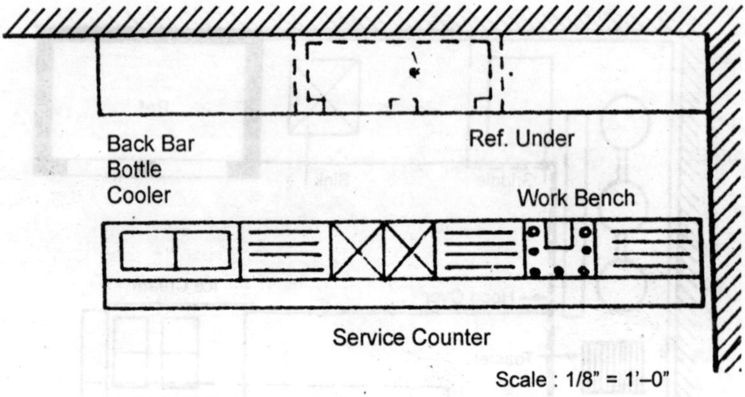

Figure 7.16: A Typical Service Bar Area.

Pot Washing Area

Figure 7.17 is typical schematic drawings indicating functional relationship for Pot Washing Area.

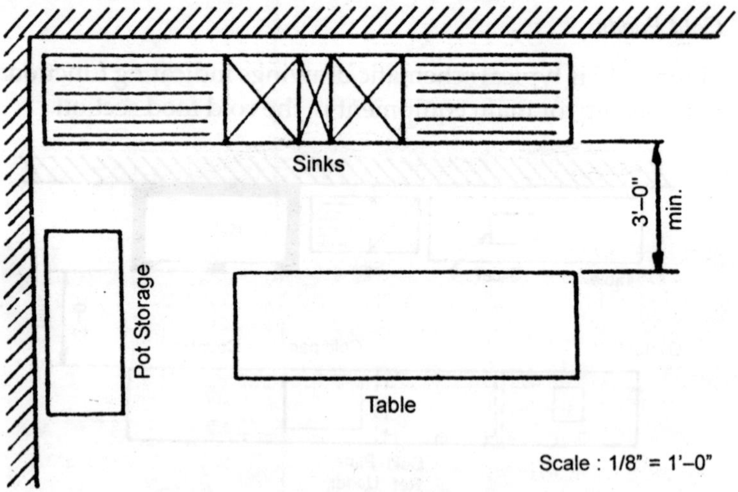

Figure 7.17: A Typical Pot Washing Area.

Dish, Glass, Silver and Tray Washing

Many types of dish and glass washers are available. Work tables may be of various shapes and designs, depending on requirement. Provide shelving marble racks soiled silverware basket, etc. as required. Sliver washers dryers and bar wishers area same time incorporated in this area. Check local codes for use of garbage grinder under scrap hole on soiled dish table. Figure 7.18 is typical schematic drainages indicating functional relationship for this section.

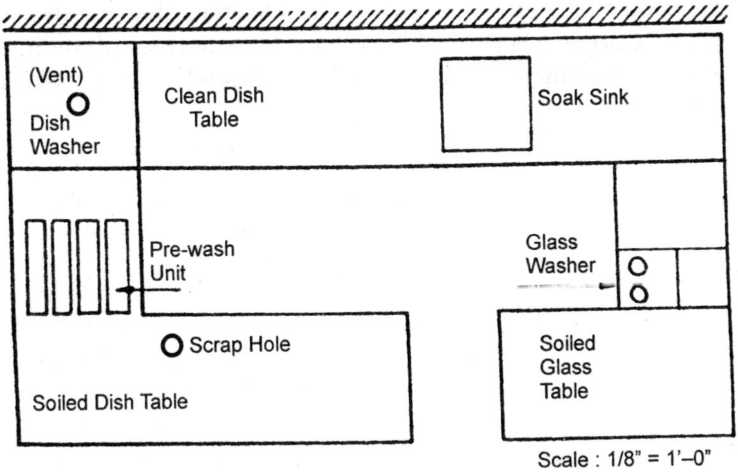

Figure 7.18: A Typical Dish, Glass, Silver and Tray Washing.

Many types o f dish and glass washers are available. Work tables may be of various shapes and designs, depending on requirements.

Provide shelving movable racks, soiled silverware basket, etc., as required.

Silver washers, dryers, and burnishes are sometimes incorporated in this area.

Check local codes for use of garbage grinder under scrap hole on soiled dish table.

Bars, Restaurants and Kitchen

You have seen schematic drawings of various kitchen areas. The drawings are intended to show efficient functional relationships of the main equipment and do not attempt to present design solutions to kitchen equipment layout.

Equipment Relationships

Types, quantity and layout of equipment will vary with anticipated patronage and menu. For example, large kitchens may need more items, such as ranges and kettles, than are shown under "Cooking Sections." Small kitchens may combine in a cooking area functions shown separately below, such as cooking and baking.

Chapter 8

Layout, Design and Facility Planning

The layout, design and facility planning directly influences employees productivity, employer's energy costs, and consumers satisfaction. The following aspects need to be considered when planning a food service facility.

1) The layout, design and facilities should be based on the selected menus and menu patterns.
2) The design should be such that future redesign and modelling is possible, facilitating new menu items and future development in equipment and machinery.
3) There should be adequate options available for the selection of various forms of energy as well as energy-efficient appliances and equipment.
4) The design and facilities (kitchen and dining room etc.) should provide for an environment in which work may be done efficiently and should lead to increased workers productivity and consumer satisfaction.

A planning team consisting of architects, engineers, interior designers, food service administration or managers can help in designing the facility.

Market and Site Analysis

Before any facilities planning is done, collect market and site analysis as given in Figure 8.1.

Market and Site Analysis Form

Date:................................ Proposed Site: ....

Type of Food & Beverage Services: ....

Characteristics: .... Comments: ....

I. *Zoning*

1) Current zoning
2) Anticipated changes in zoning
3) Height restrictions
4) Parking restrictions
5) Back and side yard restrictions
6) Sign restrictions
7) Other restrictions.

II. *Locations Drawing Time and/or Distance From*

1) Residential areas
2) Office complexes
3) Business districts
4) Educational facilities
5) Major markets
6) Sports and recreational activities
7) Historical sites and attractions
8) Inter-state highways
9) Industrial centres
10) Shopping centres.

III. *Area*

1) Type of population
2) Future growth pattern
3) Type of businesses
4) Development of nearby areas
5) Target population (s)
6) Labour outlook
7) Planned development(s).

IV. *Physical Characteristics*

1) Top soil
2) Sub-soil

(Contd.)

3) Water label
4) Surface drainage
5) Slopes
6) Landscaping
7) Elevation
8) Distance from river, creek banks
9) Other characteristics.

V. *Land Measurements*

1) Length
2) Width
3) Total area
4) Total usable area for:
   — Building
   — Parking
   — Open space.

VI. *Visibility*

1) Constructions
2) Visibility from different directions
3) Visibility of signs
4) Visibility affected by location (e.g. within a mail or a tall structure)
5) Improvements needed for visibility.

VII. *Traffic Patterns and Regulations*

1) Traffic counts on site street
2) Traffic counts on closest main street
3) Peak traffic timings
4) Type of traffic
5) Distance to nearest highway
6) Traffic regulations, one way stop signs, no-turns, speed limits
7) Parking regulations
8) Public transportation.

VIII. *Services*

1) Police
2) Fire
3) Trash
4) Garbage
5) Security.

(Contd.)

IX. *Streets*

1) Width
2) Pavements
3) Curbs
4) Side walls
5) Lighting
6) Grades
7) Hazards
8) Overall conditions.

X. *Utilities*

1) Water
2) Sanitary sewer
3) Storm sewer
4) Electricity
5) Gas
6) Steam.

XI. *Composition*

1) Number of food facilities
2) Type of facilities and menu
3) Service style
4) Number of seats
5) Average sales
6) Type of competition
7) Impact of competition.

Figure 8.1: Specimen Market and Site Analysis Form.

The Planning Process

After collecting market data and making site analysis the actual planning process should take place with an emphasis on product and consumer data. The following aspects need to be considered in the planning process:

1) Market
2) Type of menu
3) Type of operation and service:

(*i*) Speciality restaurants,
(*ii*) Fast food,
(*iii*) Industrial food service,
(*iv*) Hospital food service,
(*v*) College and university food services, and
(*vi*) School food services.

Functional Planning and Space Allocation

After completing the feasibility study, the next aspect to be considered is the functional planning. The general functions as given in Table 8.1 be broken down into various sub-functions. Each function will be carried out by performing several tasks and each one of these tasks should be considered. The next step into arrange these tasks in a way that allows a smooth and sequential flow within the area as represented in Table 8.1. These general areas are:

1) Receiving Area.
2) Storage — Dry storage, Refrigerated storage area.
3) Frozen storage areas.
4) Preparation area.
5) Production or preparation area.
6) Serving and dining areas.
7) Sanitation area.

Space required for preparation areas is based on:

1) Type of menu and items included in the menu.
2) Type of preparation and the extent of required preparation.
3) Number of items and the quality of each item to be prepared.
4) Type of service.
5) Equipment available for preparation.

Small food and beverage require relatively larger square footage per meal than those serving a large number of meals. Table 8.1 gives an idea about the average production area needed for food and beverage operation serving 300 meals.

Table 8.1: Approximate Required of Space for Food and Beverage Production Area Space Serving 300 Meals

Type of Facility	*Required Space (ft²/meal)*	*Total Space (ft²)*
Hotels	3.0-8.0	900 -2400
Restaurants	3.0-5.0	900 -1500
Hospitals	3.0-8.0	900 -2400
Cafeterias	4.0-5.0	1200 -1500
Lunch Counters	1.5-2.0	350 - 600

Once the areas for different types of preparations are planned, work spaces should be designed. The width of the worktable may range from 24 to 30 in. A work area 4 to 6 ft. long is usually convenient for an average person. Aisle spaces should be planned between work spaces. A height of 34 to 36 in is adequate for worktable. As a general rule, the equipment in the preparation area should occupy a maximum of 30 per cent of the total area.

The serving and dining areas are generally attached to preparation area with a facility of pick up center through which food is served to the customers. Space requirements for the serving and dining areas are based on the following factors:

1) Number of customers to be served per meal.
2) Type of service.
3) Largest number of customer to be served at one time.
4) Type of menu offered and accounts of customers.
5) Turnover rate of customers.
6) Type and pattern of seating arrangement.
7) Aisle spaces between seats stations
8) Number and location of service stations.
9) Table and seat sizes, shapes and numbers.
10) Special table preparation before service.

Service aisles should be about 3 ft. wide and the access aisle (for the consumers) should be 1.5 to 2.0 ft. wide. Aisles for food patrons should allow for the passage of wheel chairs. For comforts of adult would require approximately 12 ft² of space. A deluxe restaurant may require as much space as 20 ft² per person, whereas a coffee shop may allow 10 ft² per person.

Planning the Overall Atmosphere

Once the layout and design are finalised, the next step is to plan the atmosphere, taking into consideration both the future food patrons and employees. For an ethnic restaurant, special planning will be necessary to carry the ethnic theme. The following aspects should be considered in planning:

1) Appearance,
2) Odour,
3) Sound, and
4) Feeling of comforts.

All these factors in combination result in the atmosphere desired. The exterior design should also be coordinated with the inside décor. Parking areas and entrances should be attractive and should be designed to provide convenience to customers. Landscaping adds to the appeal of the facility and complements the interior atmosphere.

Design

While designing a restaurant attempt be made to relate space, décor, and other aspects into an integrated design. The main aim of planning and designing are:

1) Flexible arrangement.
2) Arranging working aisles for comfort of customers and efficiency of serving staff.
3) Minimising walking by service personnel.
4) Maximising waiter self-service by using refrigerators, hot plates and hot cupboards.
5) Sensible sequence of serving collection points.
6) Properly located and correct swinging service or kitchen doors.

Lighting and Colour Preferences

The designing of a food and beverage establishment should have versatile system of lighting. Generally bright lighting at lunch time and a diffused form of lighting in the evening is preferred. There should also be a provision to change the colour of the lights for special functions. The restaurant may select from two main kind of interior illumination—incandescent and fluorescent lighting. Special care should be taken of table lighting functional lighting restaurant surroundings, food lighting, silver, glassware and chairs on a dining table etc. There is a definite association between colour and food which need to be carefully considered pink, peach, pale yellow, clear green beige, blue and turquoise are most acceptable colours.

Furniture

Furniture needs to be chosen according to the needs of the food and beverage establishment. Chairs, floor coverings, carpets, curtains drapes, table lamps and other fittings are available in quality and design. Selection factors to be considered are:

1) Style,
2) Budget,
3) Design features such as durability, ease of cleaning, ease of storage, colour etc., and
4) Flexibility in use.

Wood, aluminium, aluminium plated steel or brass, wooden top table with metal bases, chairs with light weight metal frame and a plastic finish for the seat and the back, mica or plastic quoted table tops, plastic and fibre glass are some common varieties available.

Consider the following points when choosing the furniture and its placing, lenin, table ware, small equipment and glassware.

1) The type of clientele expected.
2) The site/or location.
3) The layout of the food and beverage service area.
4) The type of service offered.
5) The fumes available.

In addition, the other points to be considered when purchasing equipment for food and beverage service areas are:

1) Flexibility of use.
2) Type of service being offered.
3) Type of customer.
4) Design.
5) Colour.
6) Durability.
7) Ease of maintenance.
8) Stockability.
9) Costs and funds available.
10) Availability of the furniture—replacements.
11) Storage.
12) Rate of breakage i.e. China.
13) Shape.
14) Psychological effect on guests.
15) Delivery time.

Restaurant is one of the most important revenue producing area of a hotel. It requires careful planning and designing. Use a designer in a consultancy capacity relate space, décor, lighting, graphics for menus, waiting dress and other aspects into an integrated designs. Consult the waiting staff about design aspect which affect their activities. They can help assure the efficiency of design of good arrangement of seating, effective and clean maintenance and efficient service.

Proper Serving Arrangements

The designing of 'behind the scenes' or back of the house, serving arrangements must be ready to adopt rationalised procedures and should aim at:

1) Maximising walking by service personnel.
2) Maximising waiter service by using pass through refrigerators and pass through facilities at hot tables and hot cupboards.

3) Convenient sequence of serving collection points for picking up dishes, and with minimum distance for hot food to travel.
4) Properly located and correctly swing service or kitchen doors (e.g. electrically controlled doors).

Tables, Seating and Cover Space

Table size varies according to preference but does not usually exceed 760 mm (2½ ft). In some restaurant the table height is 710 m. (2 ft 4 inches). In better class restaurants, each party of customer has its own table, and two parties are never made to share. Round tables are favoured in such 'up market' operations. Larger round tables (for example, 1.75 m. diameter) may be extended by the insertion of a leaf. For popular restaurants square or rectangular tables of uniform size are generally chosen. For a high priced operations Table 8.2 gives a guidance on table sizes and seating capacity.

Table 8.2: Table Sizes and Seating Capacity

Shape	*Seating*	*Approximate Size*	
		Metres	*Feet*
Circular Table	1 person	70 mm to 750 mm diameter	2⅓ to 2 ½
	2 or 3 persons	900 m to 1 m. diameter	3 to 3¼
	4 persons	1 m diameter	3¼
	5 or 6 persons	1.25 diameter	4
	8 or 9 persons	1.50 diameter	5
	10 persons	1.75 diameter	5¾
	12 persons	2.00 diameter	8
Rectangular Table	4 persons	1.25 by 1	4 by 3¼
	6 or 8 persons	1.75 by 1	5¾ by 3¼
	8 or 10 persons	2.50 by 1	9½ by 3¼
	10 or 12 persons	3.00 by 1	9¾ by 3¼

Tables

Three accepted shapes of table are: round, square and rectangular. These tables will seat two or four people and two tables may be pushed together to seat larger parties. The size of these tables could be:

1) Round Tables

(*i*) 1 m. (3 ft.) in diameter to seat four people.
(*ii*) 1.52 (5 ft.) in diameter to seat eight people.

2) Rectangular

137 cm. × 76 cm. (4 ft. in × 2 ft. 6 in) to seat four people to which extensions could be added for larger parties.

3) Square

(*i*) 76 cm. (2 ft. 6 in.) square to seat two people.
(*ii*) 1 m. (3 ft.) in square to seat four people.

The height of the table varies a little according to preference but does not usually exceed 760 mm (2½ ft.)

Chapter 9

Determination of Room Rates

Hotels may use different methods of determination of room rates. In fact most of the hotel room rates are based on simple guess work. These hotels base their room rates on the prevalent rates charged by their neighbouring hotels, and follow an annual increase in line with inflation. However, this method is not advisable for the newly established hotels. Each hotel should establish its own rate on a more scientific basis, which is a simple task.

Rule of Thumb-Approach

Rule of thumb approach is one of the oldest and universal methods of determination of room rates. It is found that whether a hotel was built in India, Japan, London or Chicago, there is always a direct relationship between the cost of the investment in hotel property and the average room rate.

According to the rule of thumb formula, for every Rs. 10,000 spent on building, a hotel should charge Rs. 10 per room-night. For example, a hotel costing Rs. 200 lakh to build with 500 rooms gives a total cost of Rs. 4,00,000 per room. A room rate of Rs. 400 per night plus breakfast would, therefore, be appropriate.

This approach of calculating the average room rate is based on certain operating assumptions such as, that the hotel under consideration is a large unit, the average annual occupancy of the hotel varies between 65 per cent and 70 per cent and the hotel has additional income from other sources, such as food and beverage sale, store rentals, and other departmental incomes.

This approach of determining the room rates has some limitations as it does not take into account the occupancy, current rate of interest on capital, rate of inflation, the period of its application etc. All three assumptions mentioned in the formula, do not exist in the modern hotel operation. For instance, take the average annual occupancy. The annual occupancy percentage of most hotels in India does not fall in the range of 65 to 70 per cent. In most of the hotels, occupancies have been fluctuating continuously. There is no income stability in the existing hotels, and new hotels have a very modest income from their food and beverage outlets. Owing to these limitations, this rule of thumb approach is no longer relied upon as an adequate guide in the determination of room rates. However, the formula may be adopted as a starting point in case of new hotel properties.

Bottom-Up Approach

The bottom up approach to pricing is the most popular method of fixing the room rates in United States, United Kingdom, and several European countries. In this method, while preparing the profit and loss account in a vertical form, the usual practice is to start with the sale volume, deduct all the expenses and in the end arrive at the net profit required, project the expenses and in the end, arrive at the desired sales volume. This is why it is known as the bottom up approach. In brief, the bottom up procedure is explained as follows:

Step I: Determine the amount of profit aimed at. This will depend upon the profits achieved in recent years, current trends in hotel occupancies and pattern of costs behaviour.

Step II: Determine the operating costs for the next period. In case of an existing hotel, accurate projections of operating costs could be made on the basis of the past data/information.

Step III: Arrive at the required volume of room sales on the basis of the profit and operating costs.

Step IV: On the basis of estimated percentage of room occupancy, calculate the desired average room rate.

The method is clearly a profit-oriented method. It is applied with the intention to ensure that the hotel seeks adequate profitability with the right marketing context. The rates so calculated should be compared to the relevant rates charged by similar hotels.

One of the main drawbacks of the system is that in this case we assume a particular level of food and beverage departmental profit before actually determining on the level of room rates to be charged. In actual practice the volume of departmental profit secured from food and beverage operation depends, among others, on the room rates charged.

As regards to calculation of single and double room rates, there is no suitable formula available. In case the average room rate is calculated by per square footage/meter, single and double rates can easily be calculated; otherwise one will have to proceed by trial and error. Since the projected room rate is, say Rs. 500, the single room rate will be less than Rs. 500 and double rate more than Rs. 500.

Operating Cost Approach

Yet another method of calculating or determination of room rates is the operating cost basis. According to this approach, to be a profitable venture, a hotel should know its operating costs. This could be done by preparing a budget based on detailed estimates of room occupancy, overhead costs (wages, laundry costs, energy costs), variable expenses and fixed charges. The total operating costs are calculated by adding variable overheads, fixed overheads minus profit from food and beverage and other departments. An estimate is made of the net costs to be covered by sales of the room division. This is calculated by adding operating costs and profit before tax. The total number of room-nights are calculated by the following formula:

$$\text{Room Nights} = \frac{\text{Total number of rooms} \times \text{Occupancy \%} \times 365}{100}$$

The room rate is calculated as follows:

$$\text{Room Rate} = \frac{\text{Net cost to be recovered}}{\text{Rooms to be sold}}$$

The room rates for functional areas in each of the hotel are fixed in an arbitrary fashion. The cost of these areas is not given any consideration. It is advisable to take the total cost of operating the whole hotel. From the annual financial report, one can take the variable costs, fixed costs, and the amount of wages directly attributable to the banqueting department.

Thus, in this method, a budget is made on the basis of an estimated room occupancy. Overheads such as wages, laundry costs, energy costs and other variable and fixed charges are calculated. An example of this calculation is given in Table 9.1.

Table 9.1: Calculation of Average Room Rate

(Rs. in lacs)

Calculation of Operating Cost:		
Total Cost		
Fixed Costs	15.19	
Variable Overheads	114.25	
Wages (excluding F & B deptt.)	194.38	323.82
Less Profit from Food & Beverages		121.55
Operating Costs		202.27
Calculation of Room Revenue:		
Operating Costs		202.27
Profit after tax (20% on estimated investment of Rs. 925,00,000)		
Profit before tax assessment	308.33	
Less 40% tax	123.33	185.00
Estimated Room Revenue		Rs. 387.27

(Contd.)

Calculation of Room Nights:

Number of Rooms	250
Budgeted Room Occupancy	65%

$$\text{Room Nights} = \frac{250 \times 65 \times 365}{100} = 59{,}312.50$$

Calculation of Average Room Rate:

$$= \frac{\text{Room revenue to be recovered}}{\text{Rooms to be sold}} = \frac{387.27{,}000}{59{,}312.50} = \text{Rs. } 652.93 \text{ say Rs. } 653.$$

Thus, Rs. 653 is the average room rate required to produce the budgeted profit. To reach this data, the room tariff to be charged should be higher than Rs. 653. The hotel may increase this rate taking into account the prevalent market conditions.

For calculating double occupancy rate 20-25 per cent of single rate be added to this rate.

Room Rate-based on Square Footage

This method is mostly used for letting the space for offices. A hotel may also adopt this method of determining the room rate. In this method the following basic information is required:

1) Total area of bedrooms.
2) The size of each bedroom.
3) The estimated amount to produce from each room to cover overheads.

Example:

Let us assume a hotel of 250-bedrooms.

Suppose total floor area of occupied bedrooms = 50,000 sq ft. which is brokendown as follows:

Single 150 sq ft (15 m^2) × 125 = 18,750 (1,875 m^2)
Double 250 sq ft (25 m^2) × 125 = 31,250 (3,125 m^2)
50,000 (5,000 m^2)

As per the Table 9.1, the total budget revenue is Rs. 387.27 lakh, the revenue per night could be:

$$\text{Revenue per night} = \frac{3,87,27,000}{365} = \text{Rs. } 1,06,101.$$

Sales per square footage will be calculated as follows:

$$\text{Sales per sq. footage} = \frac{1,06,101}{50,000} = \text{Rs. } 2\tfrac{1}{2} \text{ per sq. ft.}$$

or

$$= \frac{1,06,101}{5,000} = \text{Rs. } 21.22 \text{ per m}^2.$$

Therefore, the rate of single and double bed will be:

Single: 150 sq. ft. × 2½ = Rs. 318
Double: 250 sq. ft. × 2½ = Rs. 530.

This could be accepted as the basis of charging the room rate.

Room Rates for Long-Term Lets/Apart Hotels

Most of the operators charge these rates on the basis of guess work, which may result in under-charging or over-charging. In case of under-charging, the owner loses the money and in case of over-charging he will lose the business. Therefore, after taking care of the relevant rent control Act/laws, following guidelines should be used in determining the room rates.

1) Determine the cost of letting a room as described above in the example.
2) Re-work the room cost figure assuming a very low profit of 10 per cent over no profit to break-even.
3) Assume that maximum booking for this type of accommodation is 25 per cent of available rooms.
4) Determine the amount for meals to be charged to cover the expenses. In cost of average meal (lunch, dinner and

breakfast), add 50 per cent to cover staff cost. Add the room rate and full board food cost plus tax, if any. The figure so calculated will be multiplied by seven in order to arrive at the weekly rate.

Calculation of Rates for Functional Areas

The rates for functional areas are fixed in an arbitrary manner. However, it is advisable to know the actual cost of functional areas and decide the rates taking into consideration the completion and the importance of the functional areas in the overall revenues of the hotel. The following procedure could be adopted:

1) Measure each functional area individually in square yard/meter.
2) Find out the percentage of functional areas to the total space of the hotel.
3) Find out the operating cost of the hotel.
4) Find out variable and fixed costs plus wages directly attributable to functional areas.
5) Charge the operating costs to the functional area on the basis of its percentage in hotel space.
6) Add a fixed percentage of hotel profit after-tax.
7) Calculate the cost per square yard for each functional area.
8) Determine the occupancy level on usage.
9) Calculate the new rate on the basis of occupancy level which will uplift the basic cost to cover the lost revenue days.
10) On the basis of competition and the importance of the functional areas in the hotel business, determine the rate to be charged.

Table 9.2: Calculation of Daily Room Rate

Suppose in a hotel there are three functional areas as follows:

Area A	1,250 sq yards
Area B	3,000 sq yards
Area C	1,875 sq yards

Fixed overheads cost of the hotel	:	Rs.194.38 lakh
Variable overheads of the hotel	:	Rs.114.25 lakh
Wages directly attributable to functional areas	:	Rs.18.75 lakh

Assuming 10 per cent of hotel profit after-tax, and 25 per cent of the hotel space is occupied by functional areas, we will calculate the daily rate for each functional area:

Total overheads for functional areas:

Total Fixed Overheads	:	Rs. 194.38 lakh
Total Variable Costs		114.25 lakh
Total Overheads	:	Rs. 308.63 lakh

25% of Rs. 308.63 lakh to functional areas	:	Rs. 77.16 lakh
Add Wages (functional areas)		18.75 lakh
Add 10% of hotel profit-after tax (assumed)		18.43 lakh
Total Overheads for functional areas	:	Rs. 114.34 lakh

Therefore, cost per square yard will be:

$$\frac{\text{Total Overheads}}{\text{Total Square Yardage}} = \frac{114,34,000}{6,125} = \text{Rs. } 1,866.78$$

Daily Rate for each Individual Functional Area

Functional Area	*Daily rate*	*Daily rates on the basis of 65% usage*
A :	$\frac{1,250 \times 1,866.78}{365} = \text{Rs. } 6,393.08$	$\frac{6393.08 \times 65}{100} = \text{Rs. } 4,155.50$
B :	$\frac{3,000 \times 1,866.78}{365} = \text{Rs. } 15,343.08$	$\frac{15,343.40 \times 65}{100} = \text{Rs. } 9,972.21$
C :	$\frac{1,875 \times 1866.78}{365} = \text{Rs. } 9,589.62$	$\frac{9,589.62 \times 65}{100} = \text{Rs. } 6,233.25$

Hubbart Formula

A formula for computing guest room rates was developed for the American Hotel and Motel Association by its financial and accounting consultants and named after Mr. Roy Hubbart, who was the Chairman of the Committee in-charge of the work. Actually, it has been used for years prior to its publication by the association in 1952. Under the Hubbart Formula, an estimate is made of the number of guest rooms to be sold in a year. Then, a tabulation is made of the cost of operation, to which is added an amount representing the expected fair return on the investment, which total amount is then divided by the number of estimated occupied rooms to obtain the average rate that must be charged. Taking into account the risk of the business, a return of 10 per cent to 15 per cent on equity capital is considered by most investors to be reasonable. Rate computed under the Hubbart Formula is best explained by the following illustration given in Table 9.3 which uses a 90-room and a 360-room hotel.

Table 9.3: Average Room Rate Computation using Hubbart Formula

	90-room hotel	*360-room hotel*
Estimate of Annual Operating Costs:		
Payroll except Catering Deptt.	Rs. 16,80,000	105,00,000
Payroll Taxes	1,25,000	8,00,000
House-keeping	6,00,000	33,00,000
Telephone	3,50,000	19,00,000
Administrative and General	5,00,000	33,00,000
Advertising and Promotion	3,60,000	18,00,000
Heat, Light and Power	3,50,000	25,00,000
Repair & Maintenance	3,00,000	20,00,000
Total Operating Expenses	Rs. 42,65,000	2,61,00,000
Fixed charges and return on Capital:		
Local Property Taxes	Rs. 3,75,000	18,00,000
Insurance on Property	70,000	3,75,000
Depreciation	14,50,000	90,00,000
Interest on Borrowed Capital	9,00,000	59,00,000
Return on Equity Investment	15,00,000	30,00,000
Total Cost and Expected Profit	Rs. 85,60,000	4,61,75,000

(Contd.)

	90-room hotel	360-room hotel
Deduct:		
Income other than Guest Room Sales:		
Profit on Catering Operations	—	85,00,000
Telephone Sales	Rs. 3,60,000	18,75,000
Store Rentals and Other Incomes	4,00,000	15,00,000
Total Credits	Rs. 7,60,000	1,18,75,000
Amount to be provided by Guest Room Sales	Rs. 78,00,000	3,43,00,000
Computation of Rent necessary to		
cover total available room per year	32,850	1,13,400
Rooms based on 70% occupancy	22,995	91,980
Net cost divided by occupied		
rooms which is an Average Rate	Rs. 1,018	1,119
Estimated Double Occupancy	50%	40%
Average Rate Per Guest	Rs.679	Rs.799
Notes on values and financing assumed:		
Original cost of building, land and equipment	Rs. 3,00,00,000	1,35,00,000
Borrowed Capital 6%	1,50,00,000	6,50,00,000
Debenture and Loan 5%	—	4,00,00,000
Equity Capital 10%	1,50,00,000	—
Equity Capital 15%	—	2,00,00,000
Average Occupancy 70%		

Determination of Hotel Room Tariffs (Rates) in India

In the years 1950's the government decided to rational the room tariff structure of hotels in the country. In pursuance of this decision a Hotel Standards and Rate Structure Committee was set up in 1957. The terms of reference of this Committee, *inter alia*, stated: "Taking into account the price level prevailing in India, the cost of hotel-keeping and other relevant factors to recommend rational rate structure for each category of hotels and other establishments."

The Hotel Standards and Rate Structure Committee submitted its report to the government in June, 1958. With regard to the hotel room rate structure, the committee observed that while each hotel determined the room tariff. taking into account the construction cost, operational costs, value of land and building, prices of commodities etc., no uniform pattern had become discernible in arriving at the room tariff. The Committee, therefore, expressed the views that it was essential that a formula be evolved for rationalising the determination of hotel room tariff. The Committee thus suggested the adoption of the Hubbart Formula followed by the American Hotel and Motel Association with appropriate modifications to suit Indian conditions. The modified formula was accepted by the Government for determining hotel room tariff in the country.

In 1962, the Government appointed a Hotel Classification Committee to classify hotels on the star category based on internationally accepted star system. For reviewing the rates charged by such hotels, as also to classify new hotels according to the star system, the Government appointed the Hotel Review and Survey Committee in 1967 with the additional objective of determining a rational basis for standardising room tariff of each category. The Committee recommended the continuance of the Modified Hubbart Formula for determining the room tariff of approved and classified hotels. Subsequently the Department of Tourism slightly amended the Modified Hubbart Formula for deleting the income-tax paid by the hotel from its operational costs.

The Modified Hubbart Formula was, thus, in operation for determining the hotel room tariff for almost 20 years. It was thus felt that a review of the formula was necessary as over the years certain ambiguities had crept in its application due to different interpretations of the Formula. For instance, in some cases the return on land and building was claimed twice, once at 6 per cent or 8 per cent on their value, and again at 10 per cent on the capital employed which also included the cost of land and building. In some cases "capital employed in hotel-keeping" was interpreted as only the working capital. To obviate such anomalies in the interpretation of the Modified Hubbart

Formula, there was a need to undertake a review of the formula, as also to examine in depth the hotel construction and operational costs for determining, if considered necessary, a new formula on which hotel room tariff could be structured.

The following points have a bearing on hotel tariff structuring:

1) Whether the return on property, viz., land and building, should be calculated on the basis of its present-day fair value?
2) Whether the return should be calculated on the historical value i.e. book value of the property after allowing for depreciation?
3) Whether in case the return was calculated on the present-day fair value of the property, interest and income-tax should be allowed as expenditure?

It is felt that the hotel room tariff formula should be based on the historical value or the book value of the property. However, those hotels operating for more than 10 years may be given an option to work out their tariff on the basis of their current fair value of the property, viz., land and building as certified by a Government approved valuer.

The return on capital invested should be adequate enough to service the loan, pay interest on it, pay dividends to shareholders, and in addition, it should help to create sufficient reserves for meeting the cost of renovations, replacements, etc., since, rapid obsolescence of equipment, decor, and wear and tear are only too frequent in the hotel industry.

Keeping all these factors in view as also the fact that hotel industry is highly capital intensive, a return of 12.5 per cent on capital invested, after deducting interest, taxation (including income-tax), and actual depreciation as claimed for income-tax purposes excluding the initial depreciation on hotel building, if any, be allowed to hotels which work out their tariff on the basis of the historical value or hook value of their property. In the case of hotels exercising the option to adopt the current fair value of the property, they may continue to be allowed, as at present, a return of 8 per cent on the fair value of the land and building as certified by a Government approved valuer and 10 per cent on the depreciated value as per rates claimed for income-tax purposes of other assets.

The following will constitute the capital employed for the purpose of claiming return on capital investment:

1) Net Fixed Assets (after charging depreciation claimed for income-tax purposes): consisting of land, building, plant and machinery, furniture, fixtures and other equipment, vehicles, etc., and
2) Current Assets minus Current Liabilities.

In view of the fact that in several cases hotels now enjoyed a high occupancy rate of over 80 to 90 per cent, it no longer appeared realistic to work out the tariff at 60 per cent as prescribed in the Modified Hubbart Formula being followed for determining the hotel room tariff. Hence, it would be more appropriate to adopt an occupancy ratio of 70 per cent for this purpose However, in order to ensure that hotels having less than 70 per cent occupancy did not suffer any disadvantage, such hotels may be given the option of taking into account the actual average occupancy of three immediate preceding completed years. Further in the case of a new hotel, the occupancy ratio may be determined on the basis of the projected or anticipated occupancy depending upon its category, location and other related factors.

New formulas may be worked out on the basis of the following common denominators:

1) The return on investment should be calculated on the fair market value/replacement value.
2) The return on investment should be linked to the operating rates of banks and not in the manner in which the properly is financed.
3) The occupancy ratio should be kept uniform at 60 per cent.
4) The ratio of single and double occupancy should be kept at 80 per cent and 20 per cent, respectively.

The background to the fixation/revision of hotel room tariff is that in accordance with the regulatory conditions prescribed by the Government, all hotels approved by it are required to fix/revise the tariff with the prior approval of the Government. This regulatory function is being performed for the last over 25 years as it was felt necessary to control tariff of hotels in India so that as a tourist destination, India's competitiveness did not get eroded in the international market.

It was discovered during application of the exisfing formula that certain provisions of the formula led to a steep rise in tariff in the case of a number of hotels. The increase was found to be far in excess of the general inflation rate in the country. During the intervening period from 1980 the revision in room tariff was allowed on ad-hoc basis. To remedy the situation, a working group was set up to have a fresh look at the formula and to suggest necessary modifications so as to remove the anomalies. The working group submitted its report in March, 1986, suggesting a new formula called the modification formula for calculation of room tariff.

The modifications recommended in the new formula cleansed the old formula of the inflationary distortions which had crept into it and were detected during the course of its actual application. However, the Federation of Hotel and Restaurant Associations of India (FHRAI) made certain suggestions in some respects and after a series of meetings between the FHRAI and the government, the modified formula for calculation of room tariff was finalised and circulated to all approved hotels. The formula has the twin objective of ensuring value for money to the customers and a fair and reasonable return on investment.

The room tariff of a hotel of the higher star category is generally more than the tariff of hotels of the lower star category located at the small place, but the formula for the fixation/revision of tariff is related to the capital structure of a hotel in that it provides for a post-tax return of 15 per cent on the capital employed (excluding borrowings) and a separate pre-tax return of 10 per cent on long-term borrowings.

Except in the case of newly completed hotels, in which case the tariff is approved with reference to its approved star category and the tariff approved for hotels of the same star category at the similar station, the revision in tariff of old hotels is allowed only once a year which remains effective from 1st October to 30th September of the following year. Table 9.4 is the modified formula for determination of the room rates in a hotel.

Table 9.4: Modified Formula for Calculation of Room Tariff

All operating and overhead expenses under appropriate heads including depreciation (excluding initial depreciation on hotel building, if any) calculated either by the written down value method as allowed by the Income Tax Act, 1961 or straight-line method as permitted by Section 205 (2)(b) of the Companies Act, 1956, subject to the condition that the method once adopted is consistently followed in the subsequent years:

Plus: Actual interest accrued for the period on all borrowings.

Plus: A net return of 15% on the net fixed assets (without revaluation) that working capital minus loans both short-term and long-term minus investment in other activities, after allowing for the national income-tax liabilities.

Plus: A pre-tax return of 10% on long-term borrowings only.

Note: Notional income-tax liability will be calculated on the basis of the rate of income-tax prescribed for the year for which tariff is being calculated. For example, if tax rate for a financial year for which the tariff is being calculated is 50% of income, the gross return on the basis of 15% pre-tax return will be 30%.

Less: Total gross revenue from all sources other than guest room sales, such as shop and storage rentals, food and beverages sales, cigarette and cigar sales, laundry and valet sales, telephone charges and miscellaneous income.

Balance: The balance is the amount to be realised from guest room sales.

Compute: Number of guest rooms multiplied by 365 days and assuming an occupancy ratio of 60%. However, in the case of hotels at hill stations and sea-side resorts occupancy ratio may be taken as the actual average annual room occupancy for the past two years or 60% whichever is less.

Option

1) Hotels more than 5 years old can claim:
   (*i*) Depreciation based on the replacement value of all

the assets of the entire property, and certified by a government approved valuer.

(*ii*) The fair market rental value as certified by a Government approved valuer in the case of rented property as an expense.

2) The replacement value of the property/market rental value once adopted will remain in force for a minimum period of 5 years.

3) Provided that:

(*i*) Hotels which follow the uniform system of accounts and can thus account for the operation of each department separately, may work out their room tariff by completely deleting the expenditure incurred and revenue earned on food and beverage operation.

(*ii*) Hotels receiving management/consultancy fees may delete the amount so earned from gross hotel revenue while computing the hotel room tariff provided the expenditure incurred on tendering such a service is also deleted from the operating and overhead expenses.

4) Determination of single and double occupancy rate That shall be determined with reference to:

(*i*) Double occupancy ratio i.e., the percentage of rooms occupied by two or more than two persons in relation to the total number of room occupied, for the year for which the figure are furnished;

(*ii*) The difference in rupees as desired between the single occupancy and double occupancy rates as related to the average room rate worked out.

Certification of Figures

The figures furnished for purposes of fixing the tariff will be supported by the following Certificate from a Chartered Accountant/Cost Accountant:

"We have verified the above statement prepared for the purpose of fixing the tariff, for the various single and double rooms in the hotel, from the books of account and certify that they are correct based upon the assumptions set out in the annexure to the statement. Further certified that wherever allocation of common expenses and/other funds are involved they are in accordance with the guidelines set in the tariff formula, if any, prescribed by the Government of India or otherwise in accordance with normal accounting practices."

Explanatory Note

1) The Operating and Overhead Expenses other than depreciation will include:

   (*i*) Consumable supplies including cost of food and beverage sales.
   (*ii*) Payroll and related expenses.
   (*iii*) Entertainment, band, music, cabaret, laundry, etc.
   (*iv*) Rent, rates, taxes, insurance.
   (*v*) Heat, light, power, gas.
   (*vi*) Repairs, maintenance and replacement.
   (*vii*) Commissions and discounts.
   (*viii*) Advertising and promotion expenses.
   (*ix*) Office and administrative expenses.
   (*x*) Directors' remuneration and meeting fees.
   (*xi*) Directors' travelling expenses.
   (*xii*) Auditors' remuneration.
   (*xiii*) Any other related expenses.

2) *Room sales*: The term "room sales" in the formula denote guest room rent only.

Allocation of Common Overheads

The Overhead Expenses of an entity that engages in activities other than hoteliering should be allocated in the proportion the Gross Revenue from such activity bears to the total turnover of the entity. The Overhead Expenses of any entity owning more than one unit of hotel should be distributed on the various operating units in the proportion, the turnover of each unit has to the total combined turnover of all operating units controlled by that entity.

Allocation of Common Loan

In case where the long-term loan for each hotel is not specifically identifiable, the total long-term loan would be allocated in proportion to the next fixed assets of each hotel.

There are two major factors which are inter-linked with the determination of hotel room tariff. These are the need to introduce an uniform accounting system for hotels, and to bring about a rationalisation in hotel design. The Government may consider:

1) Introducing the uniform accounting system in hotels on its approved list; and
2) Setting up a study group which should include an architect and an interior designer for formulating norms for the designs and construction of different categories of hotels of various sizes for ensuring optimum operational efficiency.

These measures will help to serve the interest of both the consumers and the hotels, and here again not only those of higher star category hotels in metropolitan cities, but also of hotels of all categories located at other centres in the country.

Chapter 10

Owning an Existing Hotel

In this topic we will look at some of the important points to be consideration coming to the decision to own one's own hotel. The situation need to be properly analysed to reduce the area of chance as far as possible in calculating decisions. Only experience can help in decision-making.

Acquiring the premises is apparently the first task, but three important questions should be asked:

1) Can you attract the customers?
2) Can you keep them and keep your self?
3) Do you really want to do this job?

If you can answer these questions suitably in the light of the premises in mind, then you will avoid a great deal of indecisions.

Acquiring the Premises

While acquiring the premises, remember it is the business that is being considered, not an attractive building nor an extended holiday. All difficulties need to be studied. Some of the expenses need to be considered are:

1) *The owner's salary*—as a manager a reasonable salary should be deducted before profit.
2) *Depreciation*—a figure generally missing.
3) *Interest on capital*—borrowed or not should be calculated before profit.
4) *Repairs and renewals*—include figure carefully worked out.

These are all other figures should be studied carefully. If the profit so calculated seems a fair return on capital, and the business has possible potential, and it is on the location you favour, then it is worth looking at the site.

Site

A well-known hotelier has said the site is everything. Point to consider in site selection are:

1) How far will the locality support your type of hotel?
2) What competition is there in this field?
3) What extra support may be expected, seasonally or from incoming industry, etc.?
4) Or the reverse, what lack of support will season bring?
5) Are there plans to change roads or buildings which will affect your plans?
6) Will the present customers move when you take over? In short, look around and ask, "where are they? Who?—the customers! And if you can't see them, be sure you can entice them to come.

The Building

1) The building itself is worthy of scrutiny, which way does it face? A summer exposure cuts heating bills—an exposed site can add hundreds of rupees every year.
2) And, how well is it heated?
3) Where hot water reaches the topmost bedrooms in reasonable time?
4) What is the relative site of the public rooms and the preparation room?
5) What is the storage accommodation like? You essentially require cold storage facilities.
6) Are there lots of corridors to carpet and heat?
7) Is there staff accommodation in line with your requirements?
8) Rest room and driving rooms for staff will be required?
9) What about the backyard and refuse disposal and store delivery area?

Attention to these points is required till you try to work in the hotel. Lack of support areas makes or awkward and expensive working and can aggravate the staff situation.

Essential Services

If the building seems suitable for the purpose at the moment consider the following essential services:

1) Water
2) Telephone
3) Electricity
4) Plumbing
5) Gas
6) Drainage

Have all the capacity to adop to any changes you may have in mind?

They must not be overlooked as they all are heavy cost areas, and areas which cause delay to your plans.

The Rooms

Are rooms really suitable? The dining room size, one proximity to the kitchen and bar. Lounges suitable and flexible enough for the uses you want—private parties, private meals, dances, weddings, meetings and the like. It is important that public are large enough, but not too large, and flexible enough to meet the trade you have in mind. The bedding room should also be of a suitable and careful planning to provide private bathrooms should be possible. There is a demand for rooms with private bathrooms. Some rooms you may not be able to let until alterations are done and others you will combine and divide. Can room be made connecting, are they easily accessible for the modern paying guests, or is a lift essential. Are they in short, really suitable ? It may be a better plan to keep looking if there are doubts, the next place might fill the bill better.

Guest's Comfort

Certain guests are delighted with the charm of the building and the warmth of welcomes but in the end their personal comfort will decide where they stay. Private bathrooms, lifts, central heating, television, radio and telephones in rooms tend to be taken for granted today. People can be charming about your attractive antiquity, but the majoriᴊy will find a place where modern comfort is also provided.

Alteration Required

Once you have found the premises which will be suitable after some inevitable alternations, it is certain that all essential services are there, the next step is to estimate whether a business could be viable.

A feasibility study is a reasoned guess at the future viability of the project. Use known facts as a base from which to project the costs of known or probable eventualities. It is important to do a simple calculation quickly. Its value is simply to see if there is any possibility of proceeding with this project or not.

Table 10.1: Specimen of a Feasibility of the Project

Preliminary Forecast of Capital Required Furnishings etc.				
Add:	1.	Cost of work	XXX	
	2.	Estimates of structural alterations including fees, of new installations (lifts, central heating, telephones)	XXX	
	3.	Estimates of new furnishing and fittings	XXX	
	4.	Estimates of new equipment (kitchen, pantries, bars)	XXX	
	5.	Pre-opening expenses (advertising, opening party, etc.)	XXX	XXX
Deduct:				
	1.	Sales of any surplus equipment or work	XXX	
	2.	Possible grants from time to time available	XXX	XXX
		Estimated total capital require for the project		???

Table 10.2: Forecast of Sales and Profit

	Sales	*Cost of Sales*	*Balance*
Rooms	XXX	XXX	XXX
Public Rooms	XXX	XXX	XXX
Food	XXX	XXX	XXX
Liquor	XXX	XXX	XXX
Other	XXX	XXX	XXX
	XXX	XXX	XXX
Less: Wages (A schedule of staff required should be drawn up)			XXX
			XXX
Less: Departmental expenses			
Furnishings and fittings		X	
Linen		X	
Crockery		X	
Glass		X	
Laundry		X	
Menus		X	
Staff advertising		X	
Uniform, etc.		X	
			XXX
Less: General Administration		X	
Advertising and promotion		X	
Heat, light and power		X	
Repair and maintenance		X	
Property expenses		X	XXX
			XXX
Less: Depreciation		X	
Commission given		X	
Fees		X	
Director's own expenses		X	
Room interest		X	XXX
Estimated Profit from the operation			*XXX*

Profit related to capital employed will determine whether it is worth considering the project any further.

Assuming that it is, final stage is to determine how to finance the capital and whether the cash flow allows for interest payments, and capital repayments.

Sales and Cost

No doubt it will be hoped to change the volume of sales in one way or another and this will vary the present ratio of sales from various income sources. This is called varying the sales mix. Probably price increases too will vary the volume of sales, and a useful aid at this stage is to work out what the gross income would be, assuming different prices, volume of sales and mix e.g.

Table 10.3: Schedule of Sales and Costs

Ratio of Sales	Sales	Beds at Rs.500 occupancy 40-60%	Beds at Rs.650 occupancy 40-60%	Beds at Rs.800 occupancy 40-60%
40%	Rooms	—	—	—
35%	Food less cost	—	—	—
25%	Liquor less cost	—	—	—
	Other sales	—	—	—

You may vary the ratios and prices according to possible decisions and guessing level of acceptability by the public in the form of sales and some interesting margins can emerge. It may even decide the direction of the sales effort to be in a direction contrary to first supposed selecting the most favoured ratio in—the circumstances and most likely level of sales at the chosen sales price—these can next be calculated a forecast of sales and profit.

Forecast of Sale and Profit

Get an advice from a financial accountant or an experienced hotel operator in estimating an exposure under a budget head.

Finance the Capital

Raising finance on a hotel project, other than a new building, will be difficult. Hotel operation, out of the cities, had a poor reputation of profitability and in many cases it is subject to fashion changes, population shifts, and depends to a great deal on the personality of the proprietor. For these and other reasons, Brewery companies, building societies and property companies do not welcome hotel projects. If about half of the capital employed can be put up by the proprietor, then the cash flow position is made easy as the profits after tax liability need to repay only half the capital run over possibly 10-15 years. Profits should, of course, be able to do much more than this. In the calculation to find the profit related to capital employed, a figure of around 15 per cent is not thought to be high. Do not forget tax liability in this calculation. A carefully done feasibility study which shows a better than average return will help to persuade possible lenders.

Furnishing and Equipment

Hiring furnishings and equipment has to be considered in the light of the current tax situation and with the understanding that this form of capital borrowing entails relatively heavy interest charges which results in lowering profit. In effect this will lower the return on the proprietor's capital employed in an equivalent calculation but this should be balanced against. The necessity to have the equipment to be profitable in the first place.

Functions Room

A project may require on a first priority so much in basic structured alteration and refurnishing that all available capital would be used up. As a secondary priority a function room may be considered. Leasing the furniture required instead of purchasing it may release sufficient capital to advance the creation of the function room which in turn may give a greater use of kitchen equipment currently under-used, and more economical use of staff currently on the payroll. All of these could result in high return of profit on the extra sales through the functions room which would be more than cover leasing costs of the furnishings, although themselves high. Examples of this sort show that it is very wise to turm thoughts of alternative courses of action into estimated figures as in the feasibility study. It is never time wasted.

Attract the Public

People who contemplate buying a hotel see the proposed premises as being poorly run, and as having substantial unused potential. At this stage they are generally attracted by the building or its situation and may well have an exaggerated idea of their own ability to attract customer than is there at the moment. Ask the following questions:

1) What is the present customer?
2) Why do they come?
3) Is this the market you wish to encourage?
4) What competition is there in the same market?
5) Is some other market aimed at?
6) Are there any other business in the same field?
7) Is there room to expand the chosen market?
8) Are there people within easy search who will come to you?
9) Are you sure you know their needs and are their own wants provided for in your feasibility study?
10) What, in short, is the function of your hotel, or does it have several?
11) If it has, do they mix well?
12) Can you afford to offer the services required by the chosen field of customer at the price they are willing to pay?

Atmosphere

The personality of the proprietor is one of the largest factors. There is a little point in trying to attract a type of customer with whom the proprietor and the building are out of sympathy. People like to feel at home, and they feel at have surrounded by things and people they are used to. This is always a strong likelihood that the proprietor will attract in the main people like himself and his friends. Other potential guests, no matter how good the quality and the price, tend to feel uneasy and do not come so often.

Type of Sales

Some types of trade do not mix well with others, coach trade and private car trade do not seems to mix well. A hotel doing well with one seems to do little with the others, unless in a separate part of the building. Similarly, function business in a hotel can be a disrupting influence if the flow of the traffic is through the main hall of the hotel.

A sale approach need to be carefully planned, confined to a few variety of customers as the hotel can reasonably accommodate and be priced in relation to the degree of furnishings and amenities offered, always bearing in mind what is acceptable in the region/area.

It is possible to be absolutely right in one's ideas, but if too few people agree with the ideas the venture would not be a success financially.

The Entrance Hall

Warmth of welcome is a good starting point, and a good sign and sufficient parking space are very desirable. The impact of the hall on the person coming for the first time is important and a welcome should be portrayed soft lines of the doorway perhaps broken by a plan or flowers, giving colour as well as from, cleanliness of the paintwork, and warm colour in the immediate interior are desirable.

Lighting is very important, both outside and inside the door. An open hall is more welcoming than a narrow or endorsed hall. Colour and lighting in public rooms seems to go a long way to creating an atmosphere and pictures, floral displays and ornaments will express the personality of the hotel immediately. These items or their lack, will express a personality whether planned or not. First impressions are lasting, so the entrance and shall seem to be of prime importance. Business can be attracted or repelled there.

Lighting

Lighting and colours of furnishings will tend to make the atmosphere throughout the public irony, but size of furniture, type of surfaces of tabling and materials used are also important. Comfort often portrayed in materials, shapes and colour that are not practical and a little of these materials can be used with great effect.

Use of Glass

Doorways are often forbidding. To give space and distance the use of glass is an obvious thought. Windows too can be made of and the planning of an interesting view for those using the rooms will be an attraction. Many little touches are possible to suggest distance, country, colours, sunshine, movement, and in the event of no natural attractions, some contrived attraction could be considered.

The placing of furniture to allow separate groups with a degree of intimacy is worthwhile. This can be done without any structural barrier which might add same constrain to the use of the room, so much the better.

Notices: Notices ought to be kept to the minimum, as they add a suggestion of authority which contradicts the idea of welcoming a guest. Certainly directions are required and some notices are obligatory by law, but their numbers need not be added to unduly.

Reception

An immediate meeting and verbal and visual welcome is best put over by another person, so the reception desk should be nearby, immediately recognisable and constantly manned. The correct altitude taken up the receptionist in offering a welcome is essential. The proprietor should always try to make early contract with guests too, if not actually meeting the guest personally. The personality of the business is most often judged by the altitude of the owner's and a more particularly the staff, as it cannot be expected that the owner will be there at all times.

Staffing

The personality of the owners should be reflected in the staff. It is necessary to find out availability of staff and the cost. Local staff are preferable, as staff imported from other parts of the country do not always feel happy living in a new area, no matter how congenial and rewarding the work. It is also expensive to refund travelling expenses. If staff are available, can they get to the premises ? Long walk do not appeal and running staff to buses or home is a very expensive and time consuming. The Institutes of Hotel Management, Food Crafts Institute etc., are great assets and a source of useful information. In the event of staff shortage due to illness, holidays or sheer unavailability, who can be relied upon to do the work ?

Advertising

Attracting the public is not so simple as it might appear. A careful thought to the sales approach, after consideration of the sales mix, will determine the method of selling to the customer. Advertising is a useful addition but the best advertising is by word of mouth. The staff, who should be aware of the sales approach of the owners, should be led by them to show the guests a warmth of welcome, and a willingness to serve. This concern for the guest which can only be genuine has no substitute. It is difficult to maintain this approach all the times, as hotels are open every day and for long hairs. However, once attained for a period of a year or two it tends to be self-perpetuating, and is a certain attraction to member of the public wishing to be your guests.

Staying in the Business

You as an owner has been smart enough or lucky enough—to have selected the right purchase and have it well financial, and attracted to your hotel a remunerative trade. Now, you have only one worry—to stay in business.

You have to keep making profits which are essential to be continued life of the business. Where income is rising it is sometimes overlooked that volume of trade can make the fact that the trade is unprofitable. When trade levels off somewhat, the bills and the tax collector both seem to arrive when replacement and repairs are also required. It is at this stage that business goes down the hill they have just come up.

Budgeting and Costing

The key to the problem at this stage is the careful budgeting and costing. Too often costs are ignored and selling prices are decided upon quickly, based on prices charged by the competitors. Budgeting is a similar operation to the feasibility study. It is simply an estimate of income based on prices being charged and hoped for volume, and expenses calculated in the light of reasonable assumptions of price rises, repairs required and maintenance a upgrading of property proposed during the year. Percentages given are worked out in good faith, expressing an opinion of what is reasonable at the time of writing, but it must be remembered that there are many technological changes which upset regular patterns. Items already mentioned in the forecast of sales and profit are explained with some opinion about the expected result and factors likely to affect that result.

Room Sales

Room sales do not as a rule have any cost of sales deducted from them as it is assessed that it costs nothing to let a room. In other words, it costs nothing more to let the rooms as nearly all costs have already been incurred whether the room is let or not. It is positive to isolate laundry costs and heating costs, but these costs are very small in relation to the sale. As most costs are incurred whether the room is let or not, then room sales are a particularly profitable form of sales. Same argument also applies to public room lets if these are applicable. Everyone would like to see room let to the full capacity of their beds every night, that is 100 per cent bed occupancy.

It is worth knowing, how little income you could accept from a room let in a quite time where rooms are not full. Room sales are not only most profitable in themselves, but they offer the opportunity for other sales in the restaurant or bar. As most costs are incurred any way, any income, beyond costs of laundry and cleaning increases the net profits.

Food Sales

Food sales are not always a valuable source of income. Cost of food sale is the cost of the raw products to be cooked and sold. Many hotels in order to sell their rooms keep a good table. But cost of sale in some cases have been upto 60 per cent or more of the total income. Because of the higher labour element in food sales compared with room sales, and the necessary associated expenses in the hotels, food cost must be around 40 per cent.

Cost of labour and rising on costs seem likely to make good costs a lower portion of food sales than 40 per cent in the future. In calculating a food cost as a percentage of sales, an allowance should be made for staff good. A monthly check of food cost be made. There are two many opportunities for waste, theft and fraud in this area of operation to be complacent at any time.

The most simple and accurate check is to add up total payments for food for the period, adjust for stock at the beginning and stock at the end and allow for staff food, then see what the food cost against sales is as a percentage. This should agree with the calculation on which menu prices were based, or something is wrong. This figure should be kept constantly reviewed as prices are continually changing and charges to you are not always accurate. Waste and security are constant problems.

Beverage Sales

The cost of liquor as a percentage of sales very widely. It is more profitable to sell liquors and spirits than beer, as the higher cost allows for a higher percentage profit. Public houses are expected to show a profit of about 33 per cent of total sales and more expensive cocktail bars would show a profit of about 45-50 per cent of sales, but net profit could be down by about 5 per cent.

As in kitchen, losses here can be high, due to carelessness, stealing, a fraud, and many tales of ingenious tricks. It is necessary to have an accurate check of bar stocks and income. Stocks are a great concern in the bar than the kitchen because of the high cost of vulnerability to theft. Stock kept low help to alleviate the problem.

Checking is also a little different form the kitchen, because of the direct increase of cash into the bar. To check the bar one tries to see whether all of the money which the sales of stock should have resulted in, was actually paid into the bank. This time stocks are taken at selling price as well as cost this way it is possible to calculate the amount of money which should have been drawn in for goods sold. As bar prices tend to be natural, changes in the buying prices are noted more readily and are less frequent, therefore profit from the bar does not vary much if all money is collected. It is a good plan to allow little to affect the simple calculation of stock at selling price converted into cash. For that reason a proprietor should pay cash for his own drinks and cigarettes and ensure that every other person does the same.

Cigarettes have a very low rate of profit and very high price, should be isolated from bar sales. Because of lower labour costs, bar sales even with greater cost of sales are still more profitable than food.

Other Sales

Telephone income, rent from show cases, postcard sales and so on are valuable extra source of income, but are small in comparison with main sales of the hotel.

Banqueting sales because of guide turnover and full use of facilities through large numbers, are a good sales of profit. It may be possible to lower normal charges to attract more of this type of business if it can be accommodated without annoyance to the general trade.

Expenses

Cost should be considered always in the light of the benefits received as a result of the cost. By thinking in this way a system of priorities, involves *wages cost*.

After cost of sales, wages and associated cots make up the largest area. The worker tends to look on wages as the amount received monthly, but the employer has to think of social security payment, superannuation, sickness and holiday replacements, in addition to other taxes thought up by the government departments, and of course the cost of feeding, accommodation and travel. Current costs vary between 25 per cent on low labour cost operation, e.g. bedrooms only, self-service, to 35 per cent in high cost operation, e.g. expensive restaurant.

Staff are expensive and should be used to create sales. It is a good plan to have an establishment of staff worked out in advance, with variations in busy and less busy periods as a target to work to. Consideration should be given to use of part-time workers who are only employed when helping to create sales and not at other sales.

Trained staff are cheaper than untrained staff as they normally can successfully cope with more work. Changes of staff also cause costs which are often hidden e.g. wastage, slow working, disappointment to customers through ignorance, advertising and interview costs. A good worker is worth looking after and should be recompensed in the light of what would be offered to a replacement should leave.

Heat Light and Power

This item costs over 3 per cent of income on average and can be much higher. Points to water are efficiency of the hot water plant, control through time clocks of hot water and heating, radiator controls, equipment and lights left on using electricity, continued use of heating in the kitchen and loss of heat through open doors, windows and roofs. With so much use of electrical machinery, it is difficult to keep costs in check, but it is important to know that this is main item of cost.

Laundry and Dry Cleaning

The laundry and dry cleaning in an hotel can be 2-3 per cent of income. Every effort must be made to minimise the cost through supervision of items used, use of easily washable materials, and washing small items in the hotel, repairing torn laundry to avoid total loss, more use of disposable materials is foreseen and greater use of local washing facilities.

Stationery and Telephones

Both these are fairly low cost items. Some forms of printing are very costly and buying in too large quantities does not always result in the saving. It is wise to cost menus, brochures, etc., per copy. Sophisticated system are on offer by the Telecommunication Department which greatly add to the convenience of telephones for guests and can cut down the need for a telephone operator and separate intercom-system.

Repairs and Maintenance

This is a high cost item about 2-3 per cent of sales. The use of large and costly machines seems to argue high costs. Regular maintenance is a long-term saving, and maintenance contracts seem sensible. Many firms are very quick to sell new rather than repair. Second opinions on large items are often wise and competition quotations for large expense are of work very worthwhile. It is a saving to keep paintwork in good repair, this expense is not large in relation to the customer appeal and the maintenance it offers.

Other Expenses

Other items of expenditure are fairly small by comparison and offer less scope for restricting the total cost.

Thus with six or eight budget items as regulators, costs can be kept in line with expectations or notice taken of variations.

Depreciation

Large items of equipment do wear out and replacement costs always seem to be substantially higher. Allow a reasonable figure for depreciation before calculating the profit.

Food costs and bar costs, together with wages, will account for the greater percentage of income. Particularly good control should be kept of these costs.

How to Increase Occupancy?

In most of the hotels, occupancy turns down drastically on Friday, Saturday and Sunday. As an innovative hotelier you may be able to boost weekend occupancy. One of the most rewarding sales techniques is to increase weekend business in the 'package' i.e. room meals, some extra touches for glamour at a special price.

The Vice-President of Sales and Marketing, W.W. Bud Grice says, "Getting two-thirds or half of the price of a room and meal is better than having rooms and a restaurant, empty and still having to pay salaries, utilities and taxes."[1]

A letter addressed to businessmen who have been guests previously is logical weekend profit. Direct mail letters and brochures are posted in promoting the special weekends. Newspapers, radio and TV advertising concentrates on the areas from which most guests, looking for new homes or apartments, club groups coming into the town, affluent shoppers and sports minded people (pool. sauna, tennis courts or golf courses) are drawn.

The main benefit drawn from weekend packages are:

1) Direct revenue attributable to the special weekend packages.
2) In a seasonal resort, it allows management to keep employees on year round basis.
3) Hotel shops get extra business and this in turn increases rental for them from convention managers and other sources of group business.
4) Guest for special weekends often become regular patrons and provide word of mouth advertising among their friends and associates.

The following can make positive contributions to keep occupancy high:

1) *Travel agents*

---

1. W.W. Bud Grice, Vice-President, Sales and Marketing, of a leading Hotel Company, U.S.A.

2) *Tour operators*: According to Arthur Tank, a leading tour operator, "most conventions and meetings must be sold individually and this cost money. For tours, you sell the tour operator only once and, if you attend properly to his business, you receive it year after year like an annuity."[2]
3) *Airlines*
4) *Your community*:

   (*i*) Sales manager of real business
   (*ii*) Secretaries to local executives
   (*iii*) Civic club officers
   (*vi*) Purchasing agents
   (*v*) Clergymen/religious heads
   (*vi*) Officers of women clubs
   (*vii*) Service station operators
   (*viii*) Rental car agents
   (*ix*) Bus line personnel
   (*x*) Vendors
   (*xi*) Caterers
   (*xii*) Nearby college and research centres
   (*xiii*) Attractions.

The Profession

Owning a hotel is not a past time. It is a professional job of work. The qualities required to succeed in hotel keeping could serve a person well in many other fields, most of which are less demanding and were profitable.

Generally public is very demanding master. There are so many needs to be satisfied. Some needs at times appear to the hotel-keeper to be wholly unreasonable. Guests generally expect service late in the evening or early morning and also expect the service required for early departures, but providing both can be very wearing.

The long hairs can be rising and frustration comes with the realisation that the hotel owner works hardest when others are

2. Arthur Tank, a leading Tour Operator, U.S.A.

playing holiday times, Christmas, special celebrations. This is to recognise that the work is being done freely and willingly and that pleasure and personal satisfaction come out of seeing others happy. It is necessary to accept that there will be times when disappointment comes, and it is then that other interests, out of the hotel, are necessary. Many hotelier do not involve themselves in other interests, and consequently live a difficult, closed-in life.

Disappointment

Much of the disappointment comes through staff problems, the most frequent likely to be when the most dependable help leaves because of tiredness, illness or to improve his or her income. At these times, it is worth remembering that everyone wants to advance and goodwill should be shown. The mental strain of serving the public takes a havier toll on staff than others, it is worthwhile to ensure that the rewards for the best workers do not lag behind or to allow disillusionment to set in, through sheer overwork.

Awkward Customers

Awkward customers like awkward staff are a nuisance. To look beyond the complaint and try to see the problem means that the problem can include be solved on occasions. The objective when people are difficult.

All of the foregoing analysis leads one to acceptance of a professional point of view as an hotelier, to work and plan ahead to budget and cost carefully, and to be objective to a degree about providing comfort and attention for one's guests and staff.

Professional Satisfaction

The opportunity offers the possibility of living and working in chosen surroundings, avoiding computer travel and suburban existence and, if one is successful, a comfortable income. The professional approach ensures that one brings the best out of guests, so one is normally serving pleasant people and the willingness and capability of the staff gives great help and reassurance in this. The interest of learning more about the many interesting areas involved in hotel keeping is appealing.

There is the knowledge of food and wine, each a life's study. Furnishing can provide an outlet for the artist care and maintenance of the building provides another outlet for the practically inclined. The social studies offered by contact with guests, and management of the staff is a ever ending interest.

No matter in what direction one's interest lies, there is an appeal and the satisfaction of pleasing the guest is always there. Indeed, it should always be there, as the appeal of being one's own boss will not be enough. The public is the master and in the end one has to accept this and enjoy it, as the life in Hotel Management can be very hard work if one does not. Your personal satisfaction should come from successful and profitable provision of the needs of the public, your guests, and the public is very generous in its appreciation of a warm welcome, thoughtful attention, and willing, efficient service.

Bibliography

1000 Restaurant Bar Café and Graphics: From Signage to Logos and Everything in Between by Luke Herriot.

21st Century Hotels by Graham Vickers.

Accounts and Financial Analysis in the Hospitality Industry by Jonathan A. Hales.

Asian Bar and Restaurant Design by Kim Iglis and Masano Kawana.

Asian Hotel and Catering Times, Hong Kong: Thomson Press, Hong Kong Ltd.

Asian Hotelkeeper and Catering Times, Hong Kong: Thomson Press, Hong Kong Ltd.

Best Design Wellness Hotels: North and South America, Caribbean, Mexico/Novd-Und sdumerika, Karibik, Mexico by Martin Nicholas Kunz.

Bon Appetite—Restaurant Design by A. Bokern, S. Martin Pearson, S. Moreno, and E. Vanonna.

Building Type Basics for Hospitality Facilities by McDonough.

Building Type Basics for Recreational Facilities by Richard J. Diedrich.

Building Type Basics for Retail and Mixed—Use Facilities (Building Type Basics) by The Jevde Partnership.

Business and Management Newsletter, [Hong Kong]; [Division of Business and Management Studies, Hong Kong Polytechnic].

Café and Restaurant Design by Martin Nicholas Kunz.

Catering and Hotel Management Croydon, Eng.: Blandford Business Press.

Check In; Check out Managing Hotel Operations by Juvenal J. Valley.

Compilation of Staff Research Publications. Hong Kong: The Department of Hotel and Tourism Management, Hong Kong Polytechnic University.

Conference Proceedings APAC-CHRIE Conference HONG KONG: The Hong Kong Polytechnic University.

Congress, Conventions and Exhibition Facilities by Fred Lawson.
Cool Hotels (Tools) by Aurora Cuito.
Current Awareness Bulletin for Hospitality Management, London: HCIMA.
Design and Equipment for Restaurants and Foods Service—A Management view by Costas Katsigris Thomas.
Design and Layout of Food Service Facilities by John C. Birchfield and John, Jr. Birchfield.
Design for Restaurants and Bars Inspirations for 100s International Hotels by Tina Skinner.
Design Hotels Yearbook 2007 by Design Hotels.
Designing the World's Best Resorts by Wimbery Allison Tong.
Developing Hospitality Properties an Facilities by Josef Ransley.
Developing Retail Entertainment Destinations by Michael D. Beard.
Dinning by Design: Interior Design Handbook of Dinning and Restaurant Facilities by Edie Lee Cohen and Sherman R. Emery.
Examination Papers: Full Time and Part Time Day Release Programmes. Hong Kong Polytechnic. Dept. of Hospitality Management. Hong Kong: The Polytechnic.
Exotic Retreats: Eco Resort Design by Julia Faiers.
Financial Decisions for Hospitality Decision Makers (Hospitality, Leisure and Tourism) by Chris Gilding.
HCIMA Bibliography of Hotel and Catering Management, London: Hotel Catering and Institutional Management Association.
HCIMA Reference Book Hotel, Catering and Institutional Management Association. London: Sterling Publication Ltd.
Heads in Beds: Hospitality and Tourism Marketing by Ivo Raza.
Horizons: HTM Magazine, Hong Kong: The Hong Kong Polytechnic University, Department of Hotel and Tourism Management.
Horizons: HTM Magazine, Hong Kong: The Hong Kong Polytechnic University, Department of Hotel and Tourism Management.
Hospitality and Restaurant Design, Vol. 3 by Roger Yee.
Hospitality Education and Research Journal, Washington, D.C. : Council on Hotel, Restaurant and Institutional Education.
Hotel and Restaurant Design, No. 2 by Roger Yee.
Hotel Assessment: Principles and Practices by Paul Beals.
Hotel Design, Planning and Development by Walter A. Rutes.
Hotel Front Office Management by James A. Barid.
Hotel Investments: Issues and Perspectives by Lori E. Releigh.
Hotel Management and Operation by Denney G. Rutherford.

Hotel Operations Management by David K. Hayes.
Hotel Revolution: 21st Century Hotel Design by Howard Watson.
Hotel, Restaurant, Bar, Club Design by Studio GAIA.
Hotels and Resorts: Planning and Design by Fred Lawson.
International Journal of Hospitality Management Oxford: New York: Pergamon Press.
Journal of Contemporary Hospitality Management, Bradford, England: MCB University.
Journal of hospitality & tourism research Washington, D.C.: Council on Hotel, Restaurant and Institutional Education.
Lodging …Byers guide Washington, D.C.: American Hotel and Motel Association.
Lodging and Restaurant Index. West Lafayette, IN: The Institute.
Lodging, Restaurant and Tourism Index. West Lafayette, Ind.: Restaurant, Hotel and Institutional Management Institute.
Luxury Hotels: Beach Resorts (Luxury) by Martin Nicholas Kunz.
Luxury Hotels: Golf Resorts (Luxury Hotels) by Angelika Lerche.
Luxury Hotels: SPA and Wellness Resorts by Martin Nicholas Kunz.
Managing Hotel Effectively: Lessons from Outstanding General Managers by Eddvstone C. Nebel.
Mixed-use Development Handbook by Dean Schwanke.
New Hotel Design by Otto Riewoldt.
New Perspectives: Cafes, Bars and Restaurants by Arian Mostaedi.
New Restaurant Design by Bethan Ryder.
Progress in Tourism, Recreation, and Hospitality Management London, New York: Belhaven Press.
Resort Development Handbook (Community Building) by Urban Land Institute.
Resort Management and Operation by Robert Christi Mill.
Restaurant by Design by John Riodan.
Restaurant Design by Bethan Ryder.
Restaurant Graphics by Grant Gibson.
Restaurant Planning Design and Constructing: A Survival Manual for Owners, Operators and Developers by Jeff B. Hatz.
Restaurants Clubs and Bars by Fred Lawson.
Restaurants, Cafes and Bars by Carles Broto.
Saloons and Spas: The Architecture of Beauty by Julie Sinclair Eakin.
Service Establishment: The Food Service Professional Guide 1. by Sharon L. Fullen.

Shopping Environment: Evolution, Planning and Design by Peter Coleman.
Spa and Club Design by Encarna Castillo.
Spa and Wellness Hotels (Design Pockets) by Cristina Motes.
Spas (Archi Design) by Katya Pellegrino.
Successful Restaurant Design by Regina S. Barban and Joseph F. Derocher.
The Design Hotel Yearbook 2005 by Design Hotels.
Tourism and Recreation Handbook of Planning by Manuel Baud—Bovy.
Ultimate Hotel Design by Aurora Cuito.
Ultimate Restaurant Design by Paco Asensio.

Index